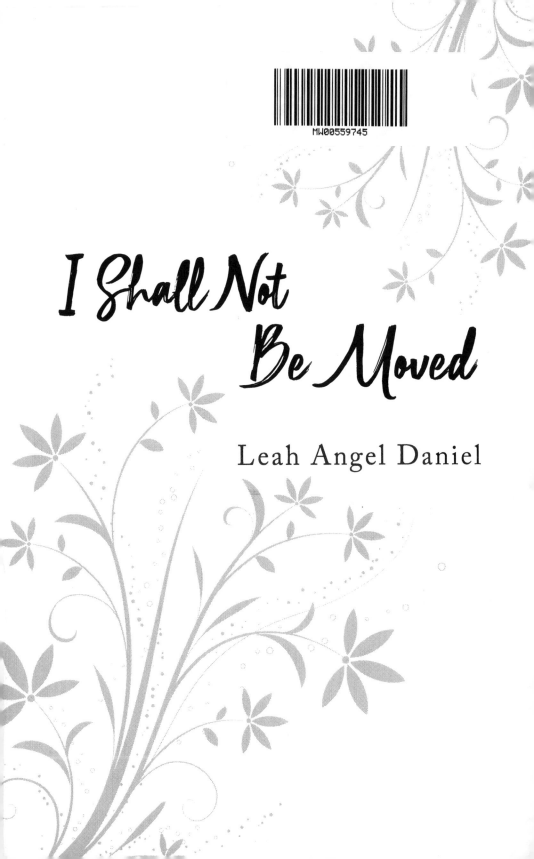

I Shall Not Be Moved

Leah Angel Daniel

13TH & JOAN

For permission requests, write to the publisher, addressed "Attention: Permissions Coordinator," 205 N. Michigan Avenue, Suite #810, Chicago, IL 60601. 13th & Joan books may be purchased for educational, business or sales promotional use. For information, please email the Sales Department at sales@13thandjoan.com.

Printed in the U. S. A.

First Printing, September 2022.

Library of Congress Cataloging-in-Publication Data has been applied for.

ISBN: 978-1-953156-83-9

Contents

Foreword

Greater Awaits for You

"Not all storms are meant for destruction, some clear paths."
∽ Ardre Orie ∾

I 've watched so many people search for the "one" thing that can change their lives for the better. We must believe that our greatest days are ahead. If we listened to the world around us, we would be led to believe that we are all in search of something different. Nothing could be further from the truth. We all desire to be loved, heard, and acknowledged. We all thirst for belonging to something greater than ourselves. We all need to experience connection on a deeper level. And while we search aimlessly for ways to engage in the human experience, the answers we seek are just beneath our noses.

The most startling revelation that I have gleaned in my life is an understanding of the power source. We have the power to change our lives and no other person, place, or thing can take this action for us. If you are reading this, rest assured that you have all of the power that you will ever need to create the life that you so desire.

Would you believe me if I told you that your power is embedded within your story? It's true. Everything you have experienced, the information you have acquired and most importantly, the moments you have triumphed prepared you for a time such as this. Understanding this concept also means claiming your power.

The hard truth is that telling your story is not always easy. There are so many factors to consider. Who will listen? Who will be inspired? Who will understand? Although important, none of these factors are of your concern. Your winning is in the resolve to set your story free. You must know that the chapter you are ashamed of writing could potentially save someone's life. This life you fought to live is an example for someone else to keep fighting.

I Shall Not Be Moved is a testament to Leah's endurance. The intricately woven set of stories sheds light on many of the trials she ultimately triumphed, leaving the world with a shining example of what it means to never give up. Leah is the personification of hope. Here words and work will leave the world with a resounding message that your story matters. The greater question then becomes... Will You Tell It?

This book is dedicated to all of the overcomers who thought that they wouldn't make it, but life worked out in their favor.

To whom much is given, much is required. This journey would not have been possible without the love and support of my village. This book has allowed me to not only share my life experiences, the good, the bad, and the ugly, but it has also provided an opportunity for me to honor the women in my family who have been overlooked, underestimated, and unprotected. I acknowledge that they endured extreme hardships so I wouldn't have to.

This book is dedicated in memory of my mother, Mercedes Jefferson-Vance, Henry "Uncle Hank" Roberts, Donez "Aunt Di' Owens, Geneva Holmes, Brenda McKenzie, Geneal "Aunt Gen" Johnson, and Dr. Theresa Harris-Tigg.

To my mentors who have stood in the gap for me, yes, I know it has been a journey, but it has been well worth it. Rose "Mama" Washington and Nellie B "Mom King, thank you for believing in me when my perspective of the world was tainted. Thank you both for praying for me, for loving me through my mess, and for being my sheroes that I needed.

To my Evangelistic Temple Community Church family and Pastor DuBois, you have all played a major role in my spiritual, educational, and life success. I love you all and appreciate everything you did to help me stay on the path to greatness.

To my sister-friend, armorbearer, and ride-or-die Tamika Potts, thank you for showing up and being who you have been to my children and me. You have blessed us beyond measure. Let your greatness shine, sis.

To my sister-friend, my sounding board Kieana Nicole Johnson, thank you for allowing me to be emotional without judgment and for helping me keep my life together. You are Buffalo's best kept secret, Kiwi. I got you!

To my siblings, I have been your second mother for the majority of your lives, and now I am looking forward to just being your big sister.

To my younger sister Clintonia Donez, I am so proud of you. Your hard work and grit astound me. Thank you for showing up and showing out when needed. I know that life hasn't been easy for you, but God has so much in store for you. Stay focused and remember God's promise to you. I love you, Mama.

To my daughters, Legend Sanaa and Jewel Penelope, you both are the greatest parts of me. Mommy loves you both to life.

To my husband, Justin Prentiss Daniel, life together hasn't been easy but I appreciate you for being what I needed when I needed it. It's time for us to grow from this point forward. I love you.

The emotional and mental rollercoaster that I experienced when writing this book was real. Thank you to my mother's lifelong friend, Sheila "Auntie Tampy" Veal, for reiterating through the process how much I meant to my mother and for helping me to understand my mother's life journey from a different perspective.

Many thanks to Ardre Orie and the 13th and Joan Publishing Company for making sure that I brought pen to paper and that this story was told the way it should be told.

Preface

Joy. Hope. Love.

I was assigned a mountain to show the world it could be moved.
～ Leah Angel Daniel ～

The lotus flower has a long and deep impact on different cultures. Throughout many civilizations, the lotus flower has taken on a significance that has meant so much to the people within global communities. For generations, the lotus flower has stood for spiritual enlightenment, resurrection, new beginnings, detachment, or purity because of how it can sprout even when in the dirtiest of environments. The flower opens its petals during the day, only to conceal them at night. It has been a spiritual plant in the past, and many individuals still hold on to those roots today. Mainly in Eastern society, people worship the lotus and appreciate it for its symbolic meaning. It's a sign of hope and new things to come. It's the hope that so many people need when wandering through life.

Introduction

Love. Strength.
Victory.

"What happens to us does not define who we become."
~ Leah Angel Daniel ~

I am the personification of the lotus flower. It symbolizes love, strength, and victory. It has the power to rise from the mud without stains. I have been a fighter all my life. Many people have trials and tribulations growing up, and I am no different. The only factor that separates me from many is that I transformed my struggle into power. From a young age, I was seen as undesirable and unwanted by both my family and the state. I was raised by a mother who was more focused on her next hit than on whether I was wearing clean clothes or not, who had babies she knew she was incapable of taking care of. If that wasn't bad enough, part of my family was no different, more worried about that drug than what their niece or granddaughter was struggling through. Once that became clear, I understood I would not have anybody on my side, which made me tough. It made me understand that if I made anything of my life, I would have to do it independently and stay focused on what was in front of me. Now I could have been driven into the same situation as my family. That would have been easy. Even when I was young, I knew if I ever wanted to try drugs, the family was the last group of people who would say no. But I decided to say no. I wanted more for myself, to be the best person I could be and make a huge impact on this world. I wanted to end the pain and hurt I was seeing in the eyes of my family members. I wanted to be one of the few people who was able to get out of their situation and make something of themselves.

When I went to foster care, I went to different homes and lived the life so many cast off as something you see in movies. I was that little Black girl who had nothing but a dream and aspirations to be more than what I saw growing up, and I became that. I am not perfect by any stretch of the imagination. I had to go through struggles even after foster care.

I became a single mom when I was young, something else I thought would never happen to me. You have to understand that statically, I was at an all-time disadvantage as a single Black mom from foster care. I was not supposed to be anything. I was supposed to be a drug addict who worked at McDonald's her whole life, but I took those adversities and made something of myself. I opened two businesses, got a college degree, and helped many people–including other young ladies in the same position I was in. It's crazy where I was and who I became. I am a testament to what you can achieve if you simply put your head down and don't let your situation at the moment determine what you will accomplish. I took every opportunity given to me because there was no other option. I knew no matter what it was, it was going to advance my life in some way. I hope to show people what they are truly capable of achieving. Don't let other people, family, or anything hold you back. We are all amazing and beautiful people in our own unique and special way. No one can tell me differently. Everyone deserves a chance and can do much more than people think. Just look at me.

I want this book to serve as a symbol of overcoming against all odds. My life is proof there is a silver lining. I could have been a victim of my circumstances, but I am not. I turned those bad times into good times. Amidst these pages, be inspired to do the same. The best investment you will ever make is in the life you dare to live.

Pillar 1:

You Are Meant For More

"Love and connection is the best thing to have with children."
∼ Leah Angel Daniel ∽

The Story

When you live a traumatic childhood as I did, you are bound to have a million memories in your head that are like puzzle pieces. Many pieces are raggedy and missing but still make a complete story. When I think of my relationship with my mom, the earliest memory that plays is when I was four, and we lived in an apartment called Town Gardens. Town Gardens was an ordinary project complex, but to me, it was a fortress. We had a big apple tree that stood strong and tall in front of our building. The tree always provided shade, which was truly appreciated when I had to sit on the concrete stoop outside. Mainly older people lived where we did. Our building, which was named McNeely Way, was quiet and clean. On this particular day, my mom was not keeping a good eye on me, which led me to bring a familiar face into our home. I was still an only child and being left to my own devices was a given. This evening my mother was in a deep sleep in her room. I remember because she was snoring horribly. She didn't wake up this one time, and I let a homeless man in our house. If you asked me how he got there, I would be none the wiser, but I remember him being in the kitchen and me feeding him and combing his hair. Being a young girl without any guidance or supervision, I guess I didn't see the dangers of my actions. He was the neighborhood drunk who I always noticed on the corner in front of the store.

Sometimes he was covered in vomit, other times he was friendly, and most of the time he was begging for money. I just always remember him being there. Eventually, my aunt came in and caught me. She was in shock. It must have tickled her to see such a sight, but she moved with caution. She casually walked to the bedroom and woke up my mother.

I heard her as she jokingly said, "Your boyfriend is in the kitchen."

My mother jumped up from her bed and burst into the kitchen to see this man on her floor. She was livid.

"You don't bring anyone into my house! He could have killed us!" Her words rang in my ears and as a young child. There was a sense of guilt that pierced me.

Looking back, how could she blame me for this? I was a completely unsupervised child. Where was her accountability and feelings of guilt for not keeping an eye on me? There wasn't any. That was my mom. She was completely void of any sense of responsibility. *I should have known better.* That was the full sentiment.

As a young girl, being disconnected from my mother was a hard pill to swallow. Every child wants to be nurtured and loved, especially by the very one they are birthed from. Unfortunately, my mother did not have that capacity. As a woman diagnosed with schizophrenia who was lost to substance abuse, many days, my mom was mean and unpleasant. None of my cousins wanted to come over, and family members did not want to interact with her because they never knew what side of her they would get. It made my childhood sad and lonely. She never spent any quality time with me. It wasn't a priority for her. Ironically, she would tell me she actually did not like kids. To hear her admit that blew my mind. How could a person who does not like children continue to have them? Her decisions only made my life more conflicting as I was forced into nurturing and caring for my younger siblings. The expectation that *I should have known better* became more concrete. Oftentimes my mother would remind me of the struggles and responsibilities she faced at my age.

I can still hear her saying, "When I was your age, I knew how to pay bills and get on the bus by myself."

As far as she was concerned, she did not get the grace she felt she needed as a child and was forced into responsibilities, so who was Leah to think she should get the grace just to be a child? Her mentality placed me in a confusing position. I was forced out of a child's place but constantly chastised for *not* being in a child's place. Many of the adults around me characterized me as grown and for knowing so much. They consequently refused to lift the burden of responsibility from my shoulders.

Being born into a family that believed I should come equipped with a "know-it-all" mentality was difficult, especially when I knew that thinking was for their benefit and not mine. When it came to taking care of my younger siblings, if I did not know what was going on or remind them of their responsibilities, the fault would be on me. One particular time I remember was my younger sister's kindergarten graduation. To any other parent or family, it would be a special time of celebration, but for my mom, it was another time to remind me that the grace of being a child was not meant for me. The day still plays sharply in my mind. My sister arrived at school with her hair disheveled in jeans and a regular T-shirt, far from graduation attire. When the school let my mom know, she turned it around on me. She shouted at me for not informing her about the graduation date. I was pissed.

"You're the adult, mom! Not me!" was all that was racing through my mind as she once again refused to take accountability for dropping the ball on her motherly duties.

It had not been the first time my mother showed her instability through my sister. On the day of their class trip to an amusement park, she sent my sister to school in a beautiful dress with her hair polished and flip-flops thinking that it was the day of kindergarten graduation. The teachers could not take it anymore. They stepped in and called Child Protective Services.

The Lesson

I gave up so much of my own childhood to watch over my siblings. It was hard because I was a child myself, and I needed an adult to show me the way and nurture me. I did not know how to do a lot of things. Though I was smart for my age, I still needed and wanted guidance. I needed to learn, and I did not have anyone to teach me. I could not help but feel that I was missing out on life as I watched my peers be teenagers while I was thrust into adulthood. It was hurtful because all I wanted to do was enjoy life. Unfortunately, my mother did not see it that way. Yet she still wanted me to be a good child who followed what she said. One day I wanted to go skating with my cousin, but my mother left my sister and me in the house. Frustrated, I contacted my aunt, who volunteered to watch my sister so I could go and act my age, at least for a night. When I returned home, I was met with an infuriated mother and a spanking.

"When I tell you to stay in this house, you stay in this house. You don't go anywhere," she said.

My heart ached in disbelief. I just wanted to go skating. I just wanted to do things that *kids* do. It was hurtful that I missed out a lot, particularly when I did not feel appreciated by my siblings. Being their older sister, many responsibilities were thrown at me. I wanted to assist them. When I worked my summer youth positions, I used the money to provide for them because they weren't being taken care of. I did not behave selfishly, and I did not pass on the ideology my mom gave of no grace for being a child. I naturally wanted to look out for them the way others did not look out for me.

When you are a child, you turn to the adults in your life to give you security and a sense of peace. Your parents are supposed to be your safe haven. For me, my mom and other family members showed me that it was easier for them to put the responsibility on me than on themselves. If they took any accountability, then it would mean they had to look deep inside themselves to uncover things they had hidden for so long. It meant they would have to work on themselves in ways they were not ready to do and see things they were not ready to see.

The Blessing

The late and great author and poet Dr. Maya Angelou once said, "I can be changed by what happens to me, but I refuse to be reduced by it."

That is me. Growing up without the nurture of my mother created a lot of painful memories and experiences. However, I decided not to live in that pain. Watching my mother gave me an opportunity to know what kind of mother *I* wanted to be. I knew that early on as a child who didn't have much choice and had situations forced on her with siblings to care for. I always told myself that when I had children, I would change the narrative. I did not want to ever put my children in a position where they had to take on responsibilities before their time because I knew how draining and confusing that is to feel as though you do not have a voice or a say in any of the things that are going on in your life. As a child, I did not have power.

I did not have anyone looking out for me to say, "That is not right," but as an adult, my power was regained. I can say, "No, that is *not* right."

I can place boundaries and speak up for myself and not be afraid of the consequences of adults.

The Lotus Pillar: You Are Meant for More

While growing up, two aspects impact how you are raised. Nature and nurture. I am the outcome of the environment I was raised in and the resilience and intuition I developed to hold my own. I always knew that I was meant for more. Even though I was not given a road map or a path, I still chose to do something different. I knew my life had more meaning than what people said I was meant for when I was younger.

When I was growing up, I was told that I was too fast and that I wasn't going to amount to anything. I wanted to show them that what they said wasn't true. I went to college and lived past the expectations people had for me. God has even exceeded the expectations I placed on myself. Being a doctoral candidate was never something I thought I would achieve. Education was something that helped me when I was younger, but I didn't expect it to take me as far as I have come. Now, I work with the foster care population.

THE AFFIRMATION

"If I am by chance changed by what happens to me, I will not allow myself to be destroyed by it."

NOTES

NOTES

Pillar 2 :

Grace Of A Daughter

"There is an opportunity for people to regain favor in the life of others."
∽ Leah Angel Daniel ∾

The Story

I know for certain in this world that you can't have anything for free, especially a place to lay your head. However, when one is at their lowest, they can only hope for someone to understand their pain. That was me. Hopeful Leah. After becoming a newly divorced single mother, I sought refuge in the one place I believed I had left–my father. My ex-husband refused to provide any assistance with our daughter, and I was out of work due to a broken wrist. There was no one else to turn to but my dad, and that is what I did. The hopeful little girl still hovering in me saw it as an opportunity to rebuild what was broken. Unfortunately, neither he nor his wife shared that vision.

I was self-sufficient for a very long time, so making the transition to depending on someone else was a hard pill to swallow. My father not being in my life the way I wanted and needed him to be was only salt added to the wounds created by my mother. I wanted this time together to be a chance for us to regain what was lost. He, as well as his wife, saw it as a chance to gain something from me. This reality was reiterated by the fact that they demanded payment for me to stay with them. Yes, I was forced to pay to stay with my father. Instead of helping the daughter in need, I was taken advantage of and had the hurt I had already experienced deepened. I was on short-term disability because of my broken wrist and received some money while waiting for my unemployment to start. I had to pay $300 a month and give them access to my food stamps card. I remember a time while being there and waiting for my lawyer to tell me what was happening with my disability and my stepmother was listening at the door.

When I was finishing the conversation with my lawyer, my stepmother came to me and said, "I heard you were getting the money from your lawyer. Can you pay me a month in advance?"

There wasn't any shame in the fact that she was eavesdropping on my conversation. She heard money was coming in, and she was certain she was going to get her share. I didn't dwell on it though, because it was her house and I was the unwelcome guest. Without any pushback, I gave her the money when I received my back pay. To my surprise, when the next month came, she accused me of not giving her a payment and demanded an extra $300 dollars. I was speechless. This lady had a lot of nerve. My saving grace was my friend, who happened to be on the phone with me at the time. She reassured me that I did indeed pay $300 the previous month. Granted, I knew that I did, but because the money was given in cash, I didn't have a paper trail. It was a relief to know that my friend was on the phone and heard everything and that the truth was on my side. She held the position I believe my father should have taken.

The Lesson

I needed my father to step in and be my hero at that moment. I was not working, regrouping from my divorce, and learning to be a new mother. I needed my father to show up for me, to be someone I could lean on without any expectations of receiving something from me in return. I needed him to be more of a father and he was not. My stepmother saw the disconnection between my father and me, and how I desperately needed his love and guidance, and she took advantage of that. She always had something to say despite the fact that I never solicited her advice. I never showed that I wanted her opinion, but she was always there to give it. Living with them emphasized that I was all alone. I didn't have anybody. I always had the mindset that if my mother and father did not do right by me, then I did not have a chance in this world with anybody else. That trust factor and feeling protected or loved to the point where no one will want anything in return is something I just didn't have with my parents. Now I have become aware of another lingering effect of my dysfunctional parental relationship. When new people come into your life and become aware that your parents have abandoned you or neglected you, they can take advantage of you. From my experience, many of them will. That was my perspective of the world. That's what happened to me.

The Blessing

In this life, there are opportunities that allow us to regain favor and love, as well as discover what was once lost. I was hoping that my father would understand this concept when I came to live with him, but he did not. We were unable to rebuild our relationship at that time, but it settled something in me. I realized I was blessed beyond measure because although my father didn't show up in the way I needed, God placed other men in my life to serve as father figures and role models. I learned at an early age that sometimes our biological parents are just the vessels for us to get here versus the ones to raise us. It's a hard truth but the reality for so many.

As a child, I was blessed with having a father figure who I called Uncle Hank. He was in my life from the time I was 12 until he passed in 2017. As a child, he was the one who picked me up for church, paid the fees for me to go on church trips, and guided me in life. He would talk to me as a father would, and he was always there for me outside of the church as well. He never missed a birthday or graduation. He was the only person I felt comfortable calling if I was in a financial bind. He co-signed for one of my vehicles. He walked me down the aisle when I got married and was there when I had my first baby. He was always present and I enjoyed being his "niece." God gave me a father figure when my own was never present. I will always be grateful for that blessing.

The Lotus Pillar

I have been raising children for the majority of my life. I never thought that I would have my own children because I knew how big the responsibility would be. I never wanted to be in a situation where my kids felt inadequate because I didn't have the proper tool kit to assist them. I have always loved my parents despite their shortcomings, but I spent more time with my mother than I did with my father. So when this opportunity came for me to live with him, I thought that it would be a time for us to get to know each other. When I moved in with him, it was the opposite. What I learned about him was that he was never going to be the father that I expected or desired. I had to deal with that harsh truth. Once I learned his story, I knew that he didn't have the capacity to do those things.

My father's mother had seven children—six boys and one girl. My father was a change-of-life-baby for my grandmother. She became pregnant with a man who was supposed to be her best friend. He was married and had no children of his own until my father was born. Although he provided financially, he was never really invested in my father's life. My grandmother compensated for what my grandfather wouldn't do, but in doing so, she began enabling my father not to be responsible. He consequently never raised any of his six children. I am the only one born out of wedlock and supposedly was the baby that was wanted, but I didn't have any different treatment than the rest of his children. My father was not there financially, emotionally, or physically. When he did show up, it was just surface-level. You could have a conversation with him, but it was never deep. He was always looking to see what he could get out of it. When we spoke or interacted with one another, I became the parent and he became the child. Our relationship was the exact same as the one I had with my mother.

Now I understand him. It doesn't hurt as bad as it did when I was a child. My father is ok with who he is. I realized that I had to move on and be the best parent that I could be to my own children. I could no longer let what I didn't have when I grew up be a hindrance.

THE AFFIRMATION

"I am deserving of love."

NOTES

Pillar 3:

In Life, There Are Cycles, Seasons, and Signs

"I could only imagine how it would feel to know that your mother gave you away and didn't want you."
～ Leah Angel Daniel ～

The Story

My grandmother gave my mother away when she was a baby to my grandfather's family. My grandmother was a heroin addict and a prostitute in and out of prison. From my understanding, my mother and grandmother didn't have the best relationship, but my mother still yearned to be close to her mom. Relatives on that side of the family were career criminals. They had a lot of money, nice clothes, jewelry, furnished apartments, and many friends. She wanted to be a part of that lifestyle, even if it meant doing things that weren't necessarily good. I was told that my mother went to my grandmother when she wanted to marry my father. She was 17, and my father was a 27-year-old pimp. I asked him if he was pimping my mom, and he replied, "Why would you ask me that?" I wanted to know. I was tired of hearing watered-down versions of how he and my mother came to be. I wanted to know his version and about him and his lifestyle. I wanted to know why he chose her. My father never truly answered my questions. I knew they met through my mother's older sister and that he was astounded by my mom's beauty and intelligence. My father thought that they would be the ultimate money-making couple. I'm told that when they decided to marry, my mother went to my grandmother to ask her to help or pay for the wedding. Supposedly my grandmother took my mother to Canada to go on a hoe stroll to earn money herself. Other family members said my grandmother didn't do that. Regardless, my mother and grandmother were like oil and water. They just did not get along. I remember my mother always called my grandmother by her first name, and my grandmother was not a grandmother to us, her grandkids. We didn't have that loving relationship that we see on television where the grandparents spoil the grandkids or even take time with them. She was not a good grandmother who my siblings or I could call and talk to on the phone or who remembered our birthday. My only memories of my grandmother are bad and include her caring more about herself than us or refusing to watch us because she felt that was too much responsibility. She had her kids already and was not interested in raising us. It was like me and my mom were a burden on her, yet my mother still tried to be a good daughter to the best of her abilities at the time. Eventually, those efforts were for nothing. Even when my mom was trying to turn her life around, she was still brought down by my grandmother despite her advanced age.

In 2000, my mother was in her late 30s, and it was my freshman year of college. She was doing good for herself, having come home from prison the previous year, clean from drugs and alcohol, and gaining back custody of my younger brothers. Then the loss of my grandmother occurred. I just remember her being in the hospital and passing away. This opened the door for my mother to start abusing drugs again. She started getting high, and I was so disappointed. It was odd to me, though. How could a person who abandoned you cause so much grief that you revert back to a lifestyle that took everything from you? My mother growing up would always say her mother was not there for her and that she didn't raise her. Aunt Gen, my grandfather's aunt, and her husband, Uncle Jack, raised my mom. They did not have children of their own. Aunt Gen and Uncle Jack loved my mom and me. Aunt Gen died from a stroke, and my mother has never been right since then. I think I was two years old then, and life became different for my mom and me. The loss made my mother cold, and she began disconnecting from everyone. Aunt Gen believed in my mom, loved my mom, and just really wanted her to do her best. That's all I ever hear from people in the family. My Aunt Jacquie is my mother's older sister on her father's side. She told me stories about how smart my mother had always been. Aunt Jacquie felt that my mom living with her paternal side of the family gave her an advantage and a better chance in life. For my mom, I am sure that was worth a million dollars. To have someone in your family tell you that you can be something beyond what you see, to support you and love you is an amazing feeling. Aunt Jacquie always reiterated that my mom didn't have to go down the same path as everyone else. My mother wanted to become a doctor. She could sing and was quite popular. She desired what any woman wanted— to be loved, adored, and cared for. To have those things and the euphoric feelings they bring, my mother was willing to do whatever she needed at all costs.

Thinking back to the day when I was 11 years old and was taken away from my mom, I was sad, angry, and confused. Now I have a better understanding of the pressure my mom was under. She didn't know how to be a mom, deal with her own issues, and move forward. When I think about my lineage and the women in my family, most of them did their best with what they had. So when I look at my mother's situation, what she was exposed to, and what she desired and yearned for from her mother, a sense of empathy begins to manifest.

These are the stories I remember that run so deep in my life. For many years people would tell me, "You're not going to be anything. You're going to be just like your mother." I thought the opposite at an early age when most young ladies desire to be like their mothers or grandmothers. I was groomed to think that my mother was bad when in reality, she had a lot of great traits that I also inherited. I heard negative things about my mother from my grandmother's side of the family. Those same relatives would also tell me that I was too fast and too grown and wanted to know too much. Most of them knew that I had never been a child and was a caretaker before I knew how to care for myself. I was so confused because I thought the purpose of my family would be to look out for me and make sure that I didn't end up in the same situation as my mom. It was just baffling to me, but what made it even worse was that I was expected to have life figured out and to know right from wrong, to make the best choices in every life scenario. How could this happen without the proper foundation? Everyone goes through life to learn, but I couldn't experience that opportunity because the expectation in my life was too great. I just kept hearing all these conflicting stories, and it was hard to decipher which was true because I could see my mom and what she was and think, "This is not good." But I have this other side of my family trying to convince me that although things looked bad at the moment, it was not always that way. My mother's lifestyle was reflective of what she went through growing up. One side of the family believed in her and tried to guide her in the right direction, while the other side taught her what they knew best, including a life of dysfunctional activities.

No one can actually tell me when my mother was introduced to her drug of choice—crack cocaine. Most of my mother's maternal family suffered from addiction. I keep thinking about how badly my mom wanted to fit in and be loved by that side of the family. As I look at old photos of them, their lifestyle looks fabulous, partying with the infamous Rick James, buying and wearing the best clothing available, and having the most exquisite vehicles to drive. I don't think that any of them ever thought that they would end up the way they have, without anything of value and even losing themselves in the process. Drugs, alcohol, boosting, and prostitution were their lifestyle, and they lived it together. My mom was the one who got hooked and could never let go. She could never recover in part because of her mental health state. Some of my family members were able to quit using drugs and learned how to live a different life.

Their mothers were drug addicts and things happened to them as a result, so they were bitter and angry as the past lingered in their present. They showed no grace to the next person or their children because they endured hardship. The pain and hurt were unresolved, allowing it to grow so big that it became uncontrollable. That's one of the saddest parts. If only someone had stepped in to protect them, guide them, and never give up on them, maybe they could have done a better job looking out for my mom.

Many of the women in my family weren't given a choice. They were groomed to be who they are today. I didn't know their stories until I began to ask in my early 20s when my mother shared so much about her life in bits and pieces. My perspective about her as a mother and person began to change. I learned how to ask the right questions: "What happened to you? Why did you live with Aunt Gen and Uncle Jack? Why are you so angry?" I learned how to engage in dialog with my mother to ask her about different things I heard from other family members, to see if she would confirm or deny stories I had been told. Sometimes she would come out and share different things. She would cry, cuss, and then laugh. I wanted to heal my mother, hold her, and tell her everything would be okay as I became an adult and saw the significance of her suffering. Her mental health was a mess, and I learned she had been diagnosed with schizophrenia. When a person uses their drug of choice, such as crack cocaine, it changes the makeup of the brain and causes a chemical imbalance. In my mother, this resulted in her being manic and violent. To see my mother in this mental health state was traumatic. She always used to say she never saw her life being like this, and I would say, "What did you want your life to be like?"

My mom had dreams and aspirations just like anybody else, but her environment didn't allow her to thrive in her greatness. Instead, she was robbed of what she could have been for herself and her children. Sadly, the lifestyle she was introduced to and chose to engage in has been the fabric of my family's generational story. No one protected me and my siblings, just like no one protected our mother. Nobody did right by her. I felt my mother's pain for the majority of my life. The remnants of abandonment, neglect, innocence snatched away, extreme expectations, little to no guidance, conditional love, and abuse defined my youth. How do these things affect a child? Sometimes they surface when the child is young but more often when they are maturing and trying to figure out life. I understood my mother. I wanted to save her, but didn't know how. I wanted to show her a different life and to know that she could rise like a phoenix, but she had to want it. She told me she enjoyed using drugs, that it was like a party for her. I just couldn't understand how she would love something that she knew was temporary, which was the major cause of her losing everything. So I watched helplessly as she lived her life the best way she knew, causing severe damage to herself and her family. Every opportunity that I had to speak life over my mother, I did it. If she were on my mind, I would check on her. If I felt she needed something to eat or whatever it was, I got it as long as it was within healthy boundaries. She knew I was her rock. I was her only consistent ally. I was no longer angry at her for not showing up as the parent I wanted her to be because I knew she just didn't have it within her to do it. I finally understood my assignment. I had a responsibility to show her a different type of love that she had never been shown before, and I was persistent.

The Lesson

Generational dysfunction is real, but generational curses can be broken. My mother spoke life over me.

She said to me, "You are the one who is going to break the generational curse. Leah, you are doing everything I was supposed to do."

I would tell her, "You got to understand the power of this moment because even though you feel like you have not succeeded. You have because I am your legacy. You have accomplished more than you know."

Growing up I didn't know what to do, but I knew I \wanted to change things. I didn't want to be like everybody else. My family suffered. I loved them and wanted the best for them, but I did not want to be like them. I didn't fit in. I didn't have role models. This was not the typical family where I had someone I connected to and aspired to be like them. The road I traveled was as lonely as it had been for my mother. Living in a constant state of wondering and putting the pieces together to see if they connected and would work was exhausting and sometimes discouraging. I just wanted to do my best and be my best.

Another thing I want you to know is that generational curses do exist. I have seen the pain and anguish it can cause with my two eyes. I know that my mother did not set out to neglect or abandon her children, but I saw how easily she fell into the same trap. I could have too. I managed to see the pattern and change my life's course. It hasn't been easy, but I've proven it is doable.

The Blessing

The biggest blessing I gained from understanding my lineage and learning about situations and circumstances that contributed to making my mother the woman she became is that I realized what I didn't want. The exposure helped me become a better mother because looking at how my grandmother treated my mom and how my mom treated me showed me how to show up better for my daughters. I was the product of the hurt they endured, and I didn't want my offspring to feel that same pain. At some point in life, someone has to say, "We gotta do better." The change starts with them. That person was me. I was determined to get out of the cycle that destroyed my family.

In a weird roundabout way, my mother used to say she had to go through this stuff in life so that I wouldn't. If my mother hadn't experienced such trauma, she would not have been the mother she was to me, and I don't know if I would have become the person I am today. Now I am far from perfect and have been through my own challenges outside my family, but when looking at my life, I can say I achieved a better outcome than most. I am not trying to glorify what I went through. I don't think anyone needs to go through pain, anguish, and heartbreak to become successful in life. If there had been another way, I would have preferred it, but I didn't have that option. I made it through with plenty of battle scars, but most people don't make it out at all.

The Lotus Pillar

I have learned that things don't always last—whether good, bad, or indifferent—and that whatever happens will not continue indefinitely. If I'm in a tough season, I try to be like a racehorse with blinders on and think about the finish line. My goal is to get through, knowing the season will change. There was a book I used to read called *Don't Die in the Winter: Your Season is Coming*. It changed my perspective on going through hardship because we can enjoy good things. I have been through years of hardship and sacrifice. In order to overcome being bitter, and appreciate the blessings that eventually come, I had to change my perspective and understand that things will not remain the same.

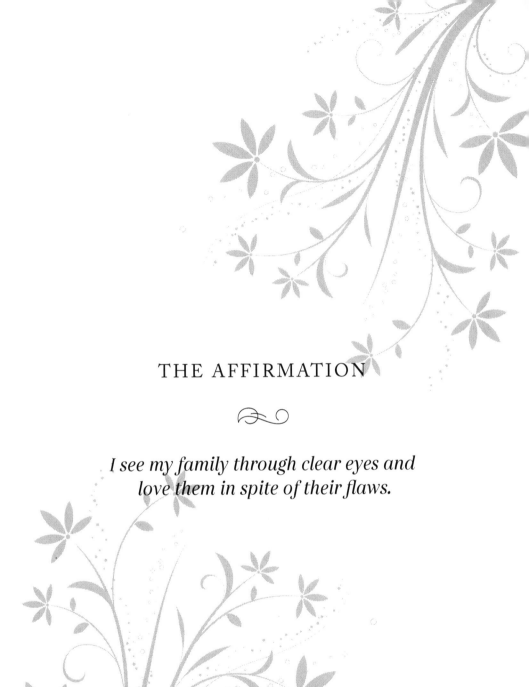

THE AFFIRMATION

*I see my family through clear eyes and
love them in spite of their flaws.*

Pillar 4:

You Will Survive

"You cannot let other people dictate how you should live your life."
Leah Angel Daniel

The Story

Once I was taken from my mom, it was very hard for me to adjust and find myself. I was in this dark place where I lacked self-esteem and self-confidence. Lucky for me, right before I went into foster care, I met Denice and Lenice, twins who went to my church. They were 10 years older than me, but I was always mature for my age, so it didn't matter. We got along fine, and they were my big sisters. I loved everything about them. They exposed me to a world that I only saw on television. They were into fashion, modeling, sewing, dancing, and hair. They were always trying to get me involved in that stuff with them. I remember they would dress me up, do my hair, and make sure I looked good for school with the latest fashions. Kids can be cruel, and I definitely did not want to become a target. The twins knew that these acts of kindness were important in my life then because, as I said, when I was taken away from my mom, I felt unworthy and less than her. The twins looking out for me gave me the confidence I needed. More than that, they were also there for me physically. They ensured I had everything I needed, which was major because I didn't get that sense of belonging and acceptance from anyone else in foster care. It also gave me a more mature mind. I was already mature as a survival mechanism. I knew I couldn't rely on anybody, and as opposed to some of the kids I was going to school with, I was dealing with real problems and didn't have the advantage of being naive.

When it came to school, I had no interest in getting to know people my age. My mindset and issues were so far above them that I was only interested in the adults there. When my sister and I went to our third foster home, I was in the sixth grade. I talked to my teachers, and they listened. I told them I was in foster care and living in a home where I was being verbally and mentally abused by my foster mother. I could not eat the food prepared by her because it made me physically ill. My sister and I could not sit on her couch, open her refrigerator, or do anything that kids typically do in their homes. We had bunk beds in the room we slept in, and we could feel the wood piercing through the mattresses. It was the worst situation imaginable. At school, there were some days I could not perform academically or keep up because I was hungry and tired, and my body was aching from the dilapidated bed. I shared these things with my two teachers, who let me have lunch with them, and we talked. They learned more about the foster care system. An assistant principal took a liking to me, so she would order food and talk to me. She even wanted to take me on as her foster child. I just remember how it felt to have adults believe in me and see things I didn't see in myself. But I think the other young people saw that I had the favor of the teachers and the vice principal, so they didn't like that. The twins Denice and Lenice dressed me nicely and taught me to care for myself. I was the new girl in school, well-dressed, and well-liked–especially by the boys. Looking back, it wasn't surprising how some of the guys treated the girls at my school. I was conversational, and they didn't all like that.

Even now, some of the people I am friends with as an adult say, "Well, you just thought you were all that, and you thought you knew everything, and we didn't like that."

From what I know about young people, instead of embracing or asking someone, "How did you do that" they get upset because they can't do what you are doing or they see the favor you are receiving. Looking back, it was all dumb little kid's stuff, but it was serious to me at the time.

I remember one of my homeroom teachers had a bowl of candy on her desk. If the class did what they were supposed to, we would get a piece of candy. One particular day, we were doing math. I had done all my work, but the class was acting up, so she said we would not get any candy.

I went up to her and said, "Ms. Drew, I was behaving, and I did my work. Can I get a piece of candy?"

She let me pick a piece. Having that influence and favor with the teachers meant other students didn't like me. The girls would call me the "teacher's pet," but I didn't care because I knew I needed the assistance of the adults to survive, and I needed them to know what I was going through. Eventually, all of the taunting and name-calling led to something physical. One girl who always had negative things to say insulted me.

I said to her, "You got as much hair on your head as I do on my privates," and she was so angry.

She said she would beat me up when we got to dismissal. She was way bigger than me, and I thought, "Oh no. I can't get beat up by this girl. What am I going to do?"

On top of that, I was still living with a foster mother who had my sister and me living in unsuitable conditions. I was tired and aching just to go to class. There was no way I was physically ready to fight anyone. My mouth got me into the situation, and I was going to see if I could talk my way out of it. So we went downstairs for dismissal. She kept taunting me. What could I say now? I was so scared that I walked up to her and punched her one good time before she had a chance to get me. It's like that age-old trick where if you get the first punch, you are more likely to win the fight. All she managed to do was pull my hair. I won that fight, despite being scared and hungry. I had to deal with the consequences of breaking school rules, but my classmates respected me. The teachers were disappointed by what I did. They knew I was better than this, and they didn't want the behavior to become routine. I didn't get in trouble with them because they knew she had been bothering me. When I think of my life transition and being in the sixth grade, I remember all the tactics I had to use to survive. Even after the physical altercation with my peer, I stayed in "go mode," not knowing what would come next. After that, for the most part, I kept to myself and didn't bother anyone.

The Lesson

The lesson from that school moment taught me that I had to be on guard and that I had to be in survival mode if I wanted to flourish in my challenging environment. I don't think there needs to be a level of fear and intimidation that a person should walk around with 24/7, but I needed to accept that I was dealing with life on my own and there were things I would have to do to survive and prove I could hold my own. We as people have a flight or fight instinct, but survival mode is different. It is an understanding of what must be done at all costs, not considering the consequences. I didn't have the luxury of caring about things other kids cared about. I didn't have that happy home with a family who fed, kissed, and tucked me in at night. I am not implying that everyone lives like that because I know they don't, but it may be hard for the people who grew up in a two-parent household and were given most of what they needed to understand what it's like to wake up every day and simply have to just figure life and hard situations out on your own without any guidance. If I could have had the chance to experience life and live carefree as a child should, I would have gladly taken it, but I didn't have that opportunity. I needed to be of an adult mind to connect with adults so that they could hear my story and maybe provide me with the foundational teachings that I lacked. Having what I needed most as a child would have made my life as I encountered exhausting trauma.

Even though it may seem like I was going through a rough time with the kids picking on me, in truth, that was what I needed to become mentally strong and learn not to react to everything someone said to me that I didn't like. I didn't care what my peers thought because they didn't live my life. That brings me to another lesson: You cannot let other people dictate how you should live your life. Those kids in my classroom didn't know anything about me. I was the new kid. They were supposed to give me a hard time. If those kids had known what I was going through, maybe they wouldn't have come at me, but my life situation was none of their business. Kids can be cruel when they know personal things about another kid and will utilize that information as bait to start some mess. I needed to do what I needed to do, and I didn't have the luxury of worrying about what other people thought about my actions or how they felt. Every day I had to go to a house with a woman who was not my mother, and she reminded me of that often. I lived under horrible conditions. That was my life as an adolescent. I didn't have time to worry about anyone else, and most people shouldn't. Life is so finite. I know that is a grossly overused cliche, but it does not change the fact that it is true. We all have real-world problems to deal with, and oftentimes when people judge you from the outside, it is an attempt to distract themselves from their own problems. Social media can do a good job of hiding it, but we all have problems.

Do what you need to do, don't worry about what the next person is doing. You need to be in survival mode at all times because I have seen too many times when it seems everything is going well, and all of a sudden, everything changes. Lucky or unlucky depends on how you look at it. I developed this mindset early in life and it has stuck with me: Put your head down and do what you need to do. Only you know your situation. Move on because that is all you can do at the end of the day.

The Blessing

This time in my life taught me I could handle myself and had people in my corner. Before the twins, I was lost. I had just been separated from my mother and lived in a roach motel. I had no clear direction at a crucial time in my childhood. With my family's history and the trauma I experienced, there was a good chance I could have chosen to go down the wrong path. When the kids started picking on me, I could have turned into that angry girl who hated everyone and got into fights every day. But I stayed true to myself, which is a life philosophy that has stuck with me.

I did not live a cookie-cutter life growing up. Things were rough from birth up until I turned 16. Without those years of struggle, I don't know where I would be. I call it character building. The bully taught me that I could defend myself when push came to shove. The teachers, assistant principal, and the twins made me realize I had people in my corner. When you are in foster care, it can feel pretty lonely. I had my sister, but sometimes family isn't enough, and you need outside influences to push you forward. Sometimes you think it's never coming your way. Those twins didn't have to help me. I was 10 years younger than them, and they could have easily just hung out with people their own age. But they embraced me, brought me up on the game, and showed me how to dress and be confident, along with other lessons I still carry with me today. My teachers and principals were important in my development because they allowed me to express my pain to them. They were the first outlet I had to reveal what was going on in my life. My principal wanted to be my foster parent, which shows the depth of our relationship. She wanted to take on the burden of having me in her life.

This was the time I realized to the smallest degree that maybe I got this. I gained confidence, which was valuable in my development. I appreciate everyone I met at this stage of my life, even the bully, because she was the catalyst who showed me what I had inside.

The Lotus Pillar

Honestly, I don't think I have ever had the option to do anything but choose to survive. My will and soul do not allow me to lie down. I am a problem-solver, so I always think about how to make a situation different. I just have an anointing. I remember a mentor, Ms. Rose Washington, who I met while I was in the foster care system. I was at the agency and only 15. She was the head directly over the foster care system I was visiting.

When she first spoke to me, she said: "You got it."

At first, I thought she was crazy, like, "What is *it*?" She saw something in me I didn't see in myself–a light I believe I have had since childhood. There were older people from my mother's paternal side of the family who believed in my mom and who raised her. I remember seeing pictures of them holding me, and I think they prayed for me because they knew my mother's lifestyle. I believe the favor of God has always been in me and with me. It's so strong that I don't even know how I have gotten through certain obstacles but through God's guidance and grace as I surrender to Him.

I always say, "Lord, give me the strength because I can not do this alone; I need you to take control," and then He surprises me and I thank Him.

One constant in my life is that God has shown up and shown out. He has taken everything I wanted to do or thought I could accomplish and turned it into something way bigger. He is the only reason that I have survived. I believed and trusted God, which is how I gained the survival tactic of changing my perspective so that I did not stay in a negative space for any length of time.

THE AFFIRMATION

"I can get through anything, no matter who tries to put me down."

NOTES

NOTES

NOTES

Pillar 5:

An Issue Too Big To Ignore

"*I had to learn how to separate myself from my family. I had to focus on my goals.*"
∽ Leah Angel Daniel ∾

The Story

Sometimes hoping for the best is what gives a person that extra push needed to not give up. It sparks a light in you that makes even the darkest moments precious. That is who my Aunt Di was for me. She was the hope a small child needed, the glimmer of light in the darkness. That was, until I moved in with her. When you live with people, you learn about who they truly are. She was my mother's older cousin, but we called her Aunt Di. I didn't know she wasn't my real aunt until I was older. When I was growing up, Aunt Di was the kind of relative who never forgot your birthday. She took you with her everywhere she went, even to bingo. She advocated for me when my mother said no. She was the aunt I felt I could trust. It did not cross my mind that she would follow the pattern of disappointment that I encountered from nearly every other adult in my life.

Moving in with her was an experience I was not ready to go through. My mother was in prison when Aunt Di took me in. I was still in foster care and this was considered kinship care because I was living with a relative. Unfortunately, she wanted me to love her more than I loved my mom. Aunt Di's behavior made me feel as if I was living with my mother all over again due to the constant babysitting and adult expectations placed on me. I was responsible for watching the younger children in the house and was not allowed to do things I wanted to do as a teenager. One Thanksgiving Eve, Aunt Di made me stay home and help cook dinner, but I wanted to go to a high school football game called the Turkey Bowl. It was an event they had every year but once again, I wasn't allowed to participate in what teenagers my age should be doing. I was furious and I let my aunt know exactly how I was feeling. Of course, she did not like what I had to say, and she let me know *that*. The women in my family are very outspoken, strong-minded, and can become violent when others say things that they do not agree with. When I told my aunt that I wanted to go to the game, she snatched me up by my shirt. Before she could do anything, my cousin interceded.

My cousin said, "Aunt Di, she didn't even do anything."

My aunt didn't agree. She didn't like that I spoke back to her and in retaliation, she called the entire family that day and told them that my cousin and I jumped her. She told them she wanted me out of her house and told me to pack my things. As far as Aunt Di was concerned, I was in her house and would follow her rules. If I didn't, then I had to leave. Because of our disagreement, she kicked my cousin out as I waited for another family member to come and pick me up. No one came so I left while Aunt Di was asleep on the couch and caught the bus to the house of my cousin who she had put out earlier. When my aunt woke up and realized that I was gone, she called my family and told everyone that I ran away. When she found out where I was, she came over, cussed me out, and tried to hit me with a phone. She threatened to put me in a group home. She was angry that I left, but I didn't care. I ended up going back to the house with her because I had nowhere else to go. While riding back in the car, she apologized to me. She said she was overwhelmed with my other siblings who were placed at her home and needed my help. She begged me to stay and help with the kids. Aunt Di said she would do better and that she knew I was getting older and needed my freedom.

It was not as if she hated me. She wanted my focus to be on her and for me to love her as my mother. Aunt Di went to any lengths to discredit my mom. She told me that my mom was probably still using drugs in prison. That statement cut me like a knife. I didn't understand why Aunt Di would say negative things about my mom. Her words discouraged me, and I felt depressed. Despite everything that was going on with my mom, I still loved her and wanted her to be in my life. I would write to my mom about what it was like living with Aunt Di, and this caused a lot of friction in the household.

I remember Aunt Di going through the mail that my mother would send and saying, "You don't tell your mother what's going on in my house. Your mother doesn't run anything over here."

I needed to believe that my mother was going to come out of prison and do the right thing. I wanted my mother to get all of her kids and do right by us. My mother and I formed a stronger relationship while she was in prison. Those were some of the most intimate moments that we shared as mother and daughter because she wrote to me about herself and her life, dreams, and aspirations. She constantly wrote about how she would make the wrong right. That image of her being healthy and responsible symbolized hope for me. I especially wanted that for my younger siblings. Even though she had lost her parental rights to me and my sister, she had the opportunity to gain custody of my younger brothers. In the end, my mother did not do as I had hoped. She got out and while she was alright for a little while, she started using drugs again at the age of 37 when her own mother passed away.

Aunt Di never took us to visit my mother in prison. I found out later that Aunt Di had her own traumatic experience when she and my mother had been in prison together in Jamaica. They had tried to smuggle marijuana into the United States. Aunt Di got caught and she flagged my mom, so they both were taken into custody. They always had a tumultuous relationship.

Drug abuse and mental health has been a plague that has haunted my family for many years. Eventually, while living at my aunt's house, a social worker came during an unexpected visit and I was removed from her custody. Aunt Di abused prescription drugs when I lived with her. I know that contributed to a lot of the issues in our relationship.

As I look back over my life now as an adult and take the time to learn my aunt's story just as I did my mom's, I understand that Aunt Di did her best. She raised me with the tools that were used to raise her. She grew up with her mother, who was the tender age of 12 when Aunt Di was born. Aunt Di did not have an essential education and was a young mother who was also exposed to a life of boosting and prostitution. She wanted to be everything to us as we grew up, but she just did not know how. Thankfully, our relationship blossomed into a more positive interaction as I grew into a young woman.

The Lesson

You can love your family members while also recognizing that you need to live your own life. My family is complex. Everyone's story is riddled with unaddressed trauma and family secrets that have yet to be healed. I have learned that there is a point in our lives when we have to focus on ourselves, and that is ok. But what does that really look like? Throughout my life, I have had to learn how to separate myself from my family. I needed to focus on my goals and recognize the things that I could not change. Boundaries were and still are made not only to create a safe space for me but to allow me to see my family's situations with fresh eyes and not judge them harshly. Everyone deserves grace, even those who are not quite ready to do the hard work that is needed to move forward.

The Blessing

Being able to love my mother despite everything she put me through is indeed a blessing. It was hard dealing with parents who were on drugs because of all that accompanies their issues, including their inability to care for their children. Neglect, abandonment, and attachment issues are just some of the things that my siblings and I dealt with due to not having our mother in her right state of mind. She was very violent when she was manic and could be nasty or disrespectful. If you didn't give her what she wanted, she would take it from you. She would be very harsh, saying cruel, hurtful, and nasty things sometimes.

I once had one of my siblings ask me, "Leah, how do you even deal with this shit? What type of mother would say these things to her kids?"

When I realized that our mother didn't have any control and what she was exposed to when she was young, her actions made sense. It was like me being in foster care. Sometimes you just want to push people away. But you can't love them out of a situation. People on the outside say it doesn't make sense and it looks dysfunctional. To those exposed to such a lifestyle, this is their reality.

The Lotus Pillar

In 2012, Aunt Di was suffering from lung cancer that later took her life. I made it my responsibility to take care of her, but my mother did not like that.

I can still hear my mother's voice as she sassed me, saying, "Why are you taking care of her for? She's not your mother."

I loved Aunt Di and just as my mother felt that I was her rock during her time of need, Aunt Di felt the same way too. They knew that I was dependable and would get the job done. I took care of business. Although Aunt Di had her issues too, she was the relative who was consistent for her nieces and nephews. Her children could not grasp the fact that their mother was terminally ill and that prohibited them from taking proper care of her. That was their trauma response, but I knew I had to be there for her. I told my mother that when it is my time to leave this earth, I want to go in comfort. I want to be surrounded by people who love me and who want nothing more for me than to make a peaceful transition. My mother had a hard time understanding that, especially considering Aunt Di's behavior when she was in jail. I had to accept how she felt and move on with what I needed to do. She may not agree with me, but I had to do what I thought was right. This was another example of how some people feel entitled to receive grace but most of the time don't want to give it in return.

When we face an issue that is too big to ignore or when reality hits us in the head and heart, we can become complacent with our situation. As much as I wanted to fix everything, I understood that I couldn't solve every problem. Recognize that you have done everything in your power and it is now time to turn off your saviorism complex. Take off the superhero cape. Respond accordingly. I have learned that I can't give more to people than they are willing to give to themselves.

THE AFFIRMATION

I am letting go of the things that I cannot control and releasing the things I cannot change.

NOTES

NOTES

NOTES

Pillar 6:

Saving Her,
Was Saving Myself

"My mother prided herself on her appearance. To see her in her current condition, I knew she was deteriorating."
~ Leah Angel Daniel ~

The Story

"I don't care, Leah. I don't want to be here anymore." That's what my mother would tell me. She would cry, lash out, and curse. She was suffering.

I witnessed my mother kill herself–not physically but mentally and emotionally. She gave up on life and the chance to do better. Honestly, she didn't even know where to start so I watched her give up on herself. I can't even describe the amount of hurt and empathy I felt when I was with her.. When I sat and talked to her, she shared how she never imagined her life would be like this. Ironically, she would admit that she enjoyed using drugs. It placed her in a position of authority that she was unable to grasp in her younger years. To her, it was a party she couldn't escape from and did not want to leave even though it slowly sucked every ounce of life from her soul. She was the life of the party and the center of attention when she utilized her drug of choice. Over the years, she deteriorated so quickly. I can vividly remember the smell of alcohol through her pores and the lack of bladder control, both of which were signs she was fading away. She no longer kept her home the way I knew she enjoyed it. Even her once beautiful teeth that she prided herself on were now broken and chipped, with some even missing. Her skin was not the same either as she had frequent black eyes and bruises. I would ask what happened.

"I fell down the stairs," she would say, but I knew better.

My mother was a fighter. She would beat up or stab anybody that she felt was a threat. She blacked out when she was on drugs and drinking. She really could sometimes not remember the altercations she had in the midst of her being manic. When her schizophrenia fits arose, she got into a lot of trouble that created destruction. I never knew what to expect. Family members and friends would call me to tell me about an incident that my mother was involved in or they would call me when it was occurring to come and pick her up. The constant anticipation of always being on guard created anxiety within me. I knew something had to give because this was not healthy and if I wasn't careful, it would be my own well-being that would be put at risk.

I was about eight months pregnant with my second daughter when my mother was hospitalized. I visited her and learned she had COPD. I remember the dark phlegm she would cough up and how her veins collapsed to the point where the only place the doctors could put an IV was in her foot. It seemed as if she was far past the point of no return, but I still saw the light. To my mother, I was her everything. Everyone knew to call me and let me know what was going on with her because I would drop everything to make sure she was alright. I was the calm to her chaos. I was her healthcare proxy and her HIPAA contact. I was the one she knew she could call on. If the doctors saw something, they reached out to me. However, no matter what I did, she wouldn't get better. Her appearance changed drastically because she no longer cared how she looked. She would bail on showing up for events and gatherings. During the time of my baby shower, she was in the hospital once again but frantically called me to get her out. The day I went to the hospital to simply visit her, I remember telling her directly,

"Look, mom, you have to get yourself together. You have so many health issues but as long as you have breath in your body, God is able to do anything."

She said "I know. I'm going to do the right thing."

She was so convincing that she pulled me in the same way she did when I was a child. She sparked my ever-present light of optimism. She appeared so excited about the baby shower, claiming she wanted to go. I remember her telling the doctor that no matter the diagnosis, she had to get out in time to make the baby shower. I believed her. In my heart, I wanted her to celebrate with me. I prepared for her to stay at the hotel with me and join me for the baby shower. She was excited that I was having another girl. The day I went to the hospital to pick her up, my all too frequent friend "disappointment" snuck up on me once again. She was gone, nowhere to be found. She signed herself out of the hospital. I could not believe it. She played me.

I called her on the phone, fueled with frustration. "Mom! You were supposed to wait!"

She had a male friend pick her up from the hospital. I could tell by the sound of her voice she returned to the life of drugs and alcohol that she enjoyed so much. She never did make it to the baby shower. I wanted her to be there. I wanted her to engage in this new life that was coming, another legacy of my mom's that I wanted her to celebrate. I wanted her to show up for my children in a way that she was not able to be there for me, but she could not even fulfill that wish. In a way, I felt bad for my mom. I wanted her to fight. I wanted her to see that she had an opportunity to get better and to do the right thing, but she did not. She did not want to. It was selfishness. At no point was she taking the time to think about how what she was doing to her life affected those who truly cared for and loved her.

The Lesson

Being everything for someone and having no one in your corner is a harsh reality. Watching my mother in the worst state of her life was gut-wrenching. I could no longer cover up her condition with the hope of the little girl lingering inside of me. The truth was the truth. I had to stand on my own two feet. I did not have any support during these different ordeals with my mother. My family simply reiterated *that* was my mother and there wasn't anything they or I could do about it. It was her life and she was living it how she wanted to. That was painful to hear. The inner- child in me needed support. I wanted my mom to be *a mother*. I wishfully wanted everything to be better than okay. I wanted to be renewed and feel whole. I needed the longing that I had to be filled. The constant reminder of having to develop my own tribe or village of people chipped away pieces of me. While I was grateful to have certain friends and individuals around me who knew the difficulty my mom and I went through, I wanted more from my immediate family. When someone you truly love is not there for you in the way that you crave, there isn't anything that can soothe that aching need or the numbness that comes with it.

The Blessing

People would call me at the beginning and end of the month to say "Your mother's out here acting up," or "Come get your mother, she is showing out."

It was hard for me to see her behave like that and to see her not care any longer. It was hard for me to see my mother deteriorate, killing herself with the things she was doing. Seeing this beautiful woman whose family thought she was going to be a doctor become unable to fully take care of herself was heartbreaking. She overdosed twice because there was fentanyl in the drugs she used. Because I loved her so much, it was hard to see her life just bleed out of her knowing who she could have been if she just fought harder. People in her family, especially on her father's side, talked about how she was when she was younger. My mother was educated, well-known for her beautiful singing voice, and she was drop-dead gorgeous. I only experienced a small percentage of the other Mercedes that my family spoke of so highly. There were only a couple of years in my life when she was not on drugs. Unfortunately my younger siblings never experienced her before her addiction. Watching her decline and pass away affected me on another level. I always yearned to have a better relationship where I didn't worry about her using alcohol or being an embarrassment. I just wanted to have a meaningful connection with her.

I did my best to empower my mother, but there was too much underlying trauma that was unresolved. Some of her many triggers were holidays, so while I knew she was sincerely interested in attending my baby shower, I also knew it was a reminder of how she could not deal with the inadequacies in her life and how she could not be there for me. Nonetheless, I understood that as much as I wanted more for her and from her, she had to want it for herself. I learned that there was no amount of love I could give that would change her. She needed to do the work for herself, but she was unwilling and I could not change that. It hurt like hell. I wanted my mother to love me and my siblings more than she loved to get high or get drunk. I wanted her to push past the pain and to fight for what could be. Even when my mother passed, I pondered the things she could have done with her life and the potential I knew she possessed. It hurts to know that she gave up on herself and on life because the pain was too overbearing to defeat. It still hurts today. My heart aches, but it has been a reality I had to accept.

The Lotus Pillar

I wanted to save my mom. Yes, my saviorism complex kicked in at full speed. Always wondering the "what ifs" and thinking "I should have done this, that or the other thing." In order to defeat the spirit of addiction, one must remove themselves from people, places, and things. This was hard for my mom because she just wanted to be loved and accepted. Don't all of us want that at some level? I felt guilty that I couldn't deliver her from the demons that plagued her mind and life. I felt as though she deserved a better quality of life. At least that was what I wanted for her before she left this earth.

I had to learn to be ok with her decisions in life. I had to set boundaries in order to love my mother but not hinder myself. I needed to love her but it didn't mean I had to let her disrespect me or take anything from me. My way of loving my mother was always keeping in communication, giving her what I could at the time, feeding her when she was hungry and sometimes even distancing myself to stay safe during her manic episodes. I would be there for her, and she knew that she could depend on me.

I can still hear her say, "Leah, a lot of what you are doing now, I was supposed to do."

While I knew she said it out of love, I also knew she was envious. I was offended in a way when she would make such comments.

However, I also understood that my mother was right. I am her legacy. I am doing everything she was supposed to do but was incapable of accomplishing because of her addiction and mental health issues. It was a catch-22 with my mother. She was indeed happy that I was evolving and elevating to do what I needed for myself but once again, I was her reminder of how she failed in her own life as a parent and as a mother. Regardless of this, I still wanted to rescue her. Many times I would think that if I moved out of town and took her with me, things would have been different. Now that opportunity will never come to pass.

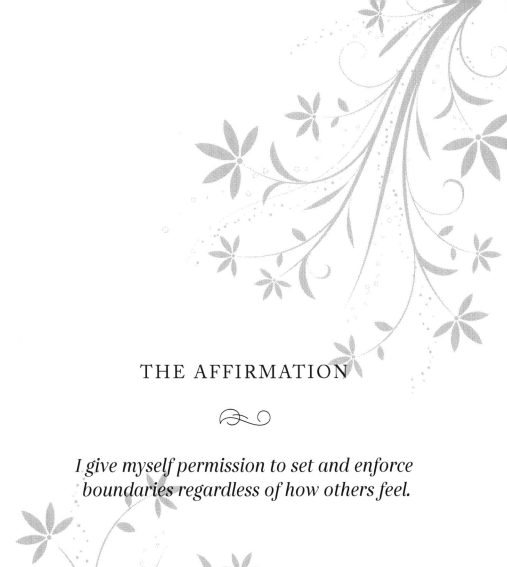

THE AFFIRMATION

I give myself permission to set and enforce boundaries regardless of how others feel.

NOTES

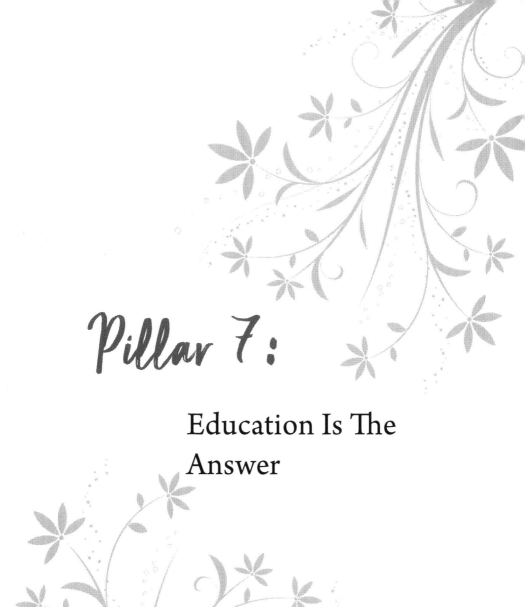

Pillar 7:

Education Is The Answer

"Don't judge others. You and the person you judge
may have more in common than you think."
∼ Leah Angel Daniel ∾

The Story

When I returned from college to Buffalo, New York, I had to readjust my career goals on top of many other challenges. I had my bachelor's degree in broadcasting and mass media and a master's degree in English. I was trying to figure out what I could do with these degrees to make good money, so I decided to start teaching introductory English courses at Erie Community College and Bryant & Stratton College. I learned through interaction with the students that the lesson plans didn't correlate with real life interactions that they needed to make for them to connect with their work. It's like what most teenagers complain about in school while learning math equations: "When am I ever going to need to use this in life?"

Unlike other teachers, I took the time to get to know my students. They came from every walk of life. One gentleman who had just taken his GED was a war veteran attending college for the first time. I asked him to write a story about what it meant to be older in college and the transitions that assisted him with his journey. When written and read, people's life transitions and journeys are remarkable stories that can profoundly impact their confidence. There were a lot of older students trying to find their way, so when I saw this routine work with the war veteran, I decided to utilize it with all of my students. This activity flourished into a business: Words Have

Wings, Healing Through Writing. I wanted everyone to feel the joy of writing about themselves that this war veteran experienced. I wanted my students to know that college was about more than *just* completing classes. My business assisted the community while allowing individuals to learn what's happening amongst their peers worldwide. As an educator, that is one of the most important things you can teach your students. Otherwise, they are memorizing information they will soon forget and taking tests with questions they will never have to worry about answering in real life. I wanted to give them an education while at the same time encouraging them to think bigger. For some, I did just that. Many people found what I was doing to be impactful in their lives. To see their faces after they finished the class was a joyous moment for me. I always knew I wanted to give back to the community that assisted me on my educational journey. When I started my business and saw what I could bring to people's lives, it felt right to me. I was in my element.

When I first started Words Have Wings, Healing Through Writing, I focused on a particular population. If a school wanted me to work with youth in an after-school program, I would learn about the student's strengths and what issues the students were having. I put together a curriculum that focused on writing to assist them with self-actualization, learning more about who they were, their beliefs, more about themselves, the origin of their names, their cultures, and different things that focused on them as individuals. I love learning, teaching, and reinforcing the importance of storytelling because it is inspirational when I hear other people's stories. I wanted to spread that to others. I had been good at learning and teaching since childhood, and people felt comfortable sharing parts of themselves with me that other people didn't care to know about.

People would often say, "I don't know why I am telling you all of my business, but I feel so comfortable and led to say these things."

I am a visionary. If someone says something about what they want to do or aspire to do, I can assist them with a strategic plan to accomplish their goal. I think people feel connected to me because of my life's calling for individuals to tell their stories. When I ask different family members or even my students about themselves, they often say no one ever asked such questions. They get excited and start sharing. All of us want to be seen, heard, and loved. I can offer those things by asking important questions, listening, and letting others know that words really do have wings. Words can break you down or build you up. I wanted the words we shared in the classroom to build up each student. I wanted the wisdom that flowed from my mouth to be a continuous reminder that everyone has a story to tell and it deserves to be told.

Starting Words Have Wings, Healing Through Writing led me to work with many different people and groups. One that stood out was working with young women in safehouses, getting them to talk about themselves and see the signals or red flags that existed on their path. Many of these young ladies were the foster care systems' products, so we connected. They felt like I was someone they could relate to. They asked me questions like "Why did you stay so long in the foster care system?" or "How did you end up in the foster care system?" Most of the time, I went to the safehouses and we had conversations that went from casual to courageous. They wanted to learn about me. They began to open up about their experiences as I provided a safe space and showed them how important they are and the significance of their stories. For them, that was major. They came from a world where their voices were probably always silenced. Some didn't even know how to tell their story. They were probably like me and in survival mode all the time. When you are in that place, certain things must be pushed to the side because you focus on making it to the next day. The stories they told me made me want to hug them tightly and tell them that everything was going to be okay. I had to hold tears back on a few occasions. I told them that this was the time and opportunity they needed to move forward and whatever they chose to be, be the best at it.

I met one young lady before working with and speaking to the youth in foster care, and I was shocked to see her there. She talked about being abused in her foster home and running away. She got involved with some guy and shared everything happening to her at that time. She made me aware of how some older women usually work with men in human sex trafficking so that they are undetected. The older women take the young ladies to stores like Victoria's Secret and find different provocative things for them to wear. There are different signs, including how women are tagged with what may look like a regular tattoo, but it shows who they belong to as the men who claim them as property. It was disheartening to learn that no one searched for her when she ran away from the foster home. What would have happened to her if she hadn't gotten away? This incident was a constant reminder of what happens to young people in foster care and the stereotype that comes with being in the system. I wanted to understand why young women, especially women of color, were devalued in a system that was supposed to help bring out their better selves. Most of the systems that we utilize in today's society are set up to do what they are doing. The system isn't broken. It is functioning very well. It is set up to help certain individuals while others are marginalized and will always be disadvantaged. That is what I am hoping to change through my work. I want everyone in the foster system to have an equal opportunity at a good life and not be brought down because of systemic racism that has developed throughout the decades. I have noticed through my efforts that the challenge of acquiring this equality is that the foster care system is already an undervalued institution, even though it has guardianship of children who have just as much potential as youth anywhere. It is going to take a complete dismantling and creative process to help all the youth affected by the foster system.

The Lesson

The girls living in the safehouses would never have told their stories if I had never worked with them directly. It was too hard, so they compartmentalized their past. They were not talking, but they trusted me and began to open up. I challenged them to think about their view of the world because of their life experiences and how things were clearer to them based on their ability to navigate life at a higher level than others. Their stories hit deeper than a dozen stories on your local news station. Listeners may have heard about the ordeals that these women who were sex trafficked had been through and would only wish for the best, but some would have preconceived notions about these girls and not take the time to understand what they have gone through. These were real people with real stories who didn't receive the resources that they needed to heal and move on with their lives. Through my program, they had an outlet to express their thoughts, fears, hopes, and dreams and they were able to be.

The people I worked with at the community colleges also had stories that helped them better adapt to the college lifestyle as adults too. We all have a story to tell. You are reading this book because you wanted to know more about mine. I hope people can learn something from what I chose to share.

The Blessing

There was a two-fold blessing from starting my business. One, I met young ladies who had been through so much. I had the opportunity to hear their stories and was reminded that I was not alone in my quest to find my "why," just as they had been. I was not alone in having life betray me as it had done them. Being around young ladies who also weren't protected motivated me to work harder, especially for little Black and Brown girls.

The other blessing focused on the individual. By coming into these young ladies' lives, I was able to provide a place of refuge for them. By allowing them to write and express their stories, I assisted them with an outlet for their emotions and an avenue to showcase their story to display how similar we all were. It was a release. I bridged a gap that enabled them to talk to each other, embrace each other's stories, and to remind them that they were all unique but had more in common than they may think. That connection was a blessing because they needed to know that they were not alone in this world. Words Have Wings, Healing Through Writing, flourished beyond those moments which touched my heart. The participation of all who chose to write and contribute made a huge difference in my life too. Each chance encounter was a blessing that just kept giving and continues to give even to this day.

The Lotus Pillar

For me, education was my pathway to success. In grammar school, the teachers, my mentors, and the assistant principal I connected with helped me accomplish what I needed to do, even after high school. College opened up a whole new world for me. I became president of the Black student union, became an AKA, was involved with many student activity groups, and learned about the world. I used to think that Africa was a place of jungles that was portrayed on PBS documentaries. But when I went to college, I met many people who were from Africa and later visited Egypt. Seeing the beauty and being able to share what Africa really looked like was an amazing experience. I lived in an international dorm, and my collegiate experiences took me beyond Buffalo, New York. My college years gave me the foresight that I needed to move beyond my circumstances and prepare for my future. I began to truly believe that I could be anything I wanted to be. All I had to do was choose. Education empowered me and allowed me to manifest a new life that I could envision for myself. It allowed me to successfully shift.

THE AFFIRMATION

I have the power to change lives with my story.

NOTES

NOTES

Pillar 8 :

Changing The Narrative

*"When you look into the mirror, sometimes that
is the only person you can rely on."*
∾ Leah Angel Daniel ∾

The Story

There was a point where I had never seen my mother and her drug addiction so bad. We didn't have food in the apartment, she left us for days, and it was like we didn't even have a mother. She was agitated all of the time. She was pregnant by the man next door, who we called Conwell. That was his last name. His sister, Ms. Virginia, also lived next door. One day she was fed up with the way my mother was raising me and my siblings. Ms. Virginia knew that my sister and I were constantly being left home alone.

She told my mother, "Mercedes, if you leave them, kids, again, I'm going to call the police."

I guess my mother didn't believe her, but when she left us again, Ms. Virginia did exactly that. Before she reached out to the police, she had us come next door to her home and she called our grandmother to see if she would take us in.

I remember her telling my grandmother, "Barbara, Mercedes hasn't been here in days. These kids are over there in that apartment by themselves. This is just not the neighborhood to have these kids being home alone. It's dangerous, and I'm about to call the police."

I will never forget what my grandmother said.

Her exact words were: "What the hell you want me to do with them, God damn kids? Call the police. Do what you gotta do. I can't take them in!"

Most people would expect their grandmother to be like their second mother in the absence of a real mother, but not our grandmother. It was like we had an absent mother and grandmother. With those odds, how would I ever expect to feel like I would be a better mother if I had children? They were my examples, or lack thereof. In the end, it did hurt to hear my grandmother say what she said, but I wasn't shocked because I was aware of who my grandmother was. This is how she showed up in our lives– null and void–and the relationship she and our mother had was tumultuous. But even then, I was like, "This is unbelievable." I had just turned 11, and my sister was 6. All we could do was wait for the police to pick us up. It was all such a huge moment. We didn't know what was going on. We just knew adults were leading us, so we needed to follow them, but from the very beginning, we didn't like any of it, or at least what we could understand.

One thing I did know was I didn't like what was happening. I remember being embarrassed and scooting down in the police car, trying to hide from anyone seeing me. I was just getting tired of always being embarrassed because of my mom, having the whole neighborhood looking at us like we were a sideshow for their entertainment and the other mothers shaking their heads, disappointed with how everything was playing out. I wanted to crawl into a hole and disappear from their prying eyes. The police officers were actually nice, even though they made me and my sister wait in the back of the car. No one in the neighborhood offered to help us out or take us in. They just peeked out their windows and pretended like they couldn't do anything for us.

The officers bought my sister and me pizza and chicken wings to make us feel more comfortable as we waited at the police station. My sister was too young to understand, but I knew to a greater extent what was happening. She just sat in the car and didn't say much. As an adult, I know that she talked about feeling invisible. My mother's children were all lighter-skinned. She was the only darker-skinned one, so she felt alienated and treated differently, like nobody wanted her. She felt like I was our mother's favorite child. Being taken away and placed into foster care didn't help with her thoughts of feeling alone and unwanted.

We were in the workout room at the police station and told to call some family members who would be willing to come to pick us up. I called a whole bunch of people, but nobody answered except my mother's father's sister, Aunt Betty. She came to pick us up from the police station, crying, saying, "I can't believe this." We drove to her house, but she did not keep us. She wanted me to talk to the social worker about seeing my mom use drugs and how she was the victim of domestic violence and an abuser herself. I trusted my great aunt, so I did what she told me to do because I thought she would keep us. She said she couldn't deal with my mother and was too old to keep my sister and me. Nobody wanted the responsibilities of dealing with our mother or us.

When the police initially took us, I felt relief from not having to go back to that neighborhood or back to my mom. Then I was scared because I didn't know anything about foster care. I didn't know what would happen, and I thought I would be in trouble because I did what Aunt Betty told me to do. My mother was mad at me and said I was the reason we were in foster care because I should have never opened the door for the police. It was a burden thrown on me because the adults didn't take responsibility or initiative for the things happening and their part in telling me what to do, so I was confused. When you live with a drug-addicted parent, there is this constant confusion because they are always gone. There is also a level of consistency in a bad way. I understood to an extent what to expect from my mother. I knew she was an addict and would go missing for days at a time. Foster care was a different environment that I knew nothing about.

The first foster home we went to was with Ms. Retha Hunter, a phenomenal foster mother. Unfortunately, she had breast cancer and passed away, so we only lived with her from August to December. We didn't know what would come next, but we already had that initially good experience. That first house set my sister and me up for failure. We had a certain expectation of what a foster home would be. There was also the lonely aspect of it all. Let's just say that was the beginning of a turbulent decade-plus of my life.

The Lesson

The experience of entering the foster care system made me wonder what a true family was. People feared my mom and didn't want to take responsibility for us because of her violent outburst. My family members were like the people in our neighborhood the day we were taken to the police station, acting as if they were helpless. I had my great aunt and my grandmother turn their backs on my sister and I because they didn't want to be burdened with caring for two kids with an absent mother. That whole situation just left a bad taste in my mouth. They could have helped us, but they didn't, which is why the events in my life played out the way they did.

I don't want to seem bitter, but I was left questioning where the family members that claimed they tried to get us before we went into foster care were. That festering enragement followed me through most of my adolescence and young adult life. I was mad at everyone. In my eyes, they were all fake and phony. When I would question certain family members about why they didn't get my sister and me, they would make up some lame excuse or would tell me something I would later find out wasn't true. It was just a very confusing time.

I had family members who loved me and wanted the best for me, but when I was put into a situation where I needed them to help me, they didn't. I was crushed. I learned at an early age that no one would look out for me more than I did myself. I realized that not long after I went into foster care, that's when I began to live in survival mode fully. I had to do what I needed to do to ensure that my sister and I were safe while trying to figure out how to get out of our current situation.

I don't want people to see their families as I saw mine. Everyone wasn't the same, but the majority of them were. I know many people who have loving families. I commend all of the families who operate in love and as a unit. The events in my life taught me that there can be variations in families and how they love one another. I love my family and to this day, I honor the stories that they have shared with me.

The Blessing

The blessing of this moment in my life was being placed in the foster care system. I experienced things that I would not have if I had not been in foster care, both good and bad but all life-changing. Being a part of the foster care system was not easy or fun. I would much rather have been in a family with a mom who was not addicted to drugs and emphasized my development. I didn't get that. I had to learn at an early age how to navigate life and think as an adult, live within my means, and how be mentally strong. I don't know if I would have had that level of growth or survival strategy if I had continued to live with my mom or even my grandmother or great aunt. Foster care toughened me to the realities of life. It taught me valuable lessons that I hold onto today. When I lived with my mother, I was in a constant state of fight, flight, or freeze. I didn't understand my strength until I was placed in foster care.

Here is another reality: If I had stayed with my mom or family members, there is a great chance that I would have ended up in the same situation as the majority of my family members. Misinformed, misled, misguided and messed up. My chances of following that path would have been much higher. The foster care system showed me I needed to grow up fast and look after myself and my brothers and my sister as much as possible. I was the oldest and much was expected from me. The foster care system exposed me to the other ugliness of life. Most of the foster parents I lived with were not the best, but I expected that type of behavior from them. I was not their blood and they didn't owe me anything. Their cruel behavior indirectly taught me how to grow up and to be smart about what moves I made, what I did, and how I operated in life. Being a young Black woman in the foster care system was another giant to tackle. The inadequacies that I experienced enhanced the mission that I lead today to assist foster care youth, young adults and alumni, especially those of color who are transitioning out of the foster care system. My experiences made me want to operate a business, spread my message, and improve the outcomes for those exiting the foster care system. It made me want to become a proud contributing member of society and crush the stereotypes pointed my way. Would I have had these ambitions if I had never gone to foster care? I don't know what or who I would have become. In the end, I didn't prefer to be in foster care, just as I didn't want my parents to be negligent or to abandon me, but I can say that these occurrences of my life made me into the woman that I am today.

The Lotus Pillar

We don't get to choose our family. For a long time, I was ashamed of who my family was, but as I grew into an adult, I developed an understanding of who I am, who my mother was, and her lineage. I began to understand that all families are different. I just wanted to take what I could from my relatives and turn all the negativity into something positive. I embraced it all. Looking back, the women in my family were courageous, strong, by-any-means-necessary types of women despite the adversities they faced. They were beautiful, boisterous, and assertive. I wanted to emphasize all that they had accomplished, whether big or small and all they had survived. Instead of looking at their deficiencies and struggles, I focused on their dreams, aspirations, what they accomplished, and how they all deposited in my life despite being subjected to the titles placed on them for their life decisions. I just stopped focusing on that and more on the other things they brought into my life and the lives of others.

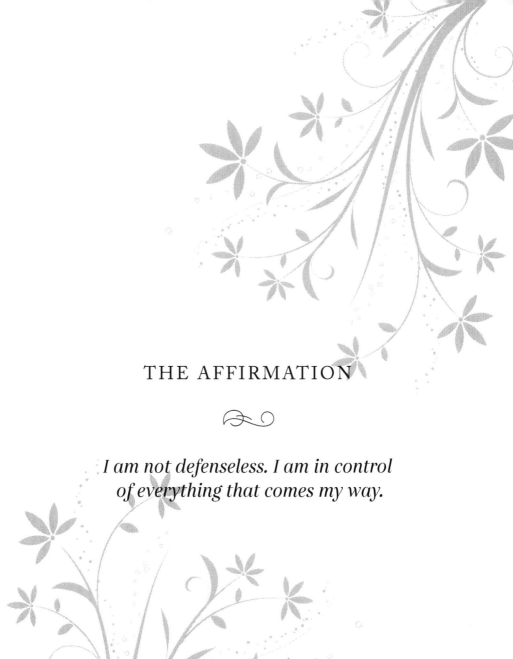

THE AFFIRMATION

*I am not defenseless. I am in control
of everything that comes my way.*

NOTES

NOTES

NOTES

NOTES

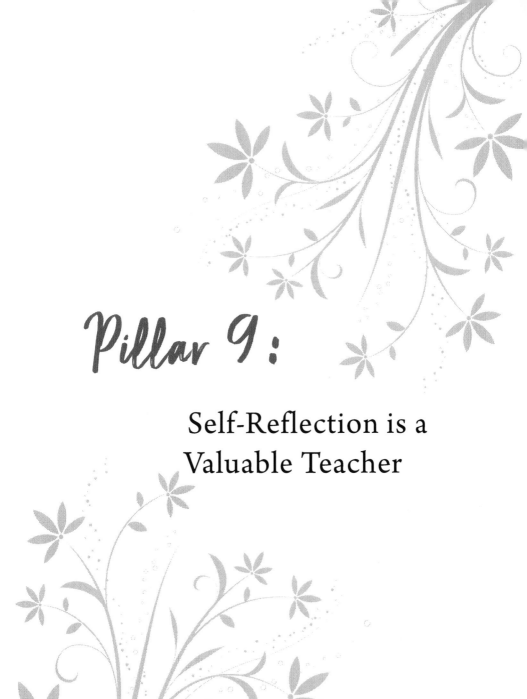

Pillar 9:

Self-Reflection is a Valuable Teacher

*"When I think back on what they did, they showed
me what I didn't want to become."*
~ Leah Angel Daniel ~

The Story

A conventional family, like the ones you may see on TV, was far from anything my mother or I was born into. For generations, my family decided that a lifestyle of hard work and a 9-to-5 schedule was not part of what they envisioned for themselves. I saw pictures of my parents riding in Bentleys and dressed in fur coats. There was even a picture of them with Rick James. It appeared they had a rich and luxurious life, and I wanted to know more about it. I wanted to learn how they went from luxury to despair. What I discovered was far from fabulous. My family had whorehouses. Yes, whorehouses. They invested in prostitution. They filled homes with beautiful Latina and Black women who knew how to get anything from a man. They would use what they had to get what they wanted. My mother saw that life of luxury and wanted that lifestyle. There wasn't anything her father's family could do to stop that. They tried their best to prohibit her from going down such a path, but she did what she wanted to do. It went downhill from there.

As I gained small amounts of information on my mother's life, I wanted to know more. My inquisitive mind could not help but question, "*What happened to her?*" I realized that the answer was drugs. Drugs took away her capabilities and potential to walk in her greatness as a successful woman and, more importantly, as a mother.

I always would ask my aunts as well, "What made my mom use drugs?"

I never got a straight answer. They told me many different reasons. They would say she had a lot of traumatic things happen to her. She was molested while visiting her mother's side of the family. Her mother's mother, who she did not like, did not stop what happened and continued to keep it a family secret. My mother didn't feel protected or loved. She did anything that she could to get the recognition of family members. She started using the same drugs most of them used. Even two days before she passed away, she was bothered by how relatives were talking about her even though they were all doing the same thing. My mom just really wanted someone to love her. I think about how deep her stories were and a lot of the things that she shared. I realized that she had to be willing to give up something, but she wasn't. She had to be willing to go for help and go to rehab, but she just couldn't. I remember asking her why she would sacrifice everything in her life for drugs, and she told me that it was like a party. She just had to be there, and it was fun. She expressed how she got that one hit and just continued chasing that high while nothing else mattered. It just made me want to grab her, hug her, and tell her it would be okay.

I told her, "As long as you have breath in her body, you have another chance to make your life what you want it to be."

God gave her another chance, but she didn't believe that and was just worn out. Right before she passed away, she constantly said she was tired and just wanted to die. I would ask her why she said that and tell her it hurt me. I was always trying to extract different things from her and see what was true and what wasn't. I asked other family members about her being molested.

The response I would get was, "Oh, I did hear about that. Her grandfather on her mother's side molested her."

I found out when I started asking questions that a lot of the females were molested on that side of the family, and no one did anything. Many of them still went into prostitution. They devalued themselves and to this day, they continue to carry that trauma. My mom always told me that I broke the generational curse and did everything that she was supposed to do. I used to be offended a little bit when she said that because they didn't give me everything that I needed. They didn't push me to go to college, and none of them did anything to help me become successful. What they did do was show me what I didn't want to become. Not that I was judging them, but it scared me so bad. I saw the outcome, and I told myself that I didn't want to be like them. I didn't know what I wanted to be, but I knew I didn't want to follow their path. On the outside, looking in, my family was dysfunctional, but the question was, how do I tell that to a family that thinks that these things are normal? That is their way of life. They had an abundance of things in their past lives, but they were not educated or literate. Now they have nothing.

The Lesson

Self-reflection is a valuable tool. When I reflect back on my child-hood, I am able to see that the shortcomings of my parents weren't always their fault. They had their own trauma that prevented them from being who I needed them to be. Knowing the full story enabled me to contemplate the past in a way that I would never have been able to previously. My mother used drugs and drank alcohol exces-sively to cope with her own trauma. My family struggled because of the precedent set by previous generations. At times in your life, have you ever wondered why something bad is happening to you? Have you ever blamed yourself for the pain that was inflicted on you? Only when one steps away and reflects can they see that it was never really personal but rather the result of trauma and dysfunction that was passed down generation after generation.

The Blessing

Overcoming is always an option when you are alive. God has given us the gift of life and second chances. We can always begin again, and that is a great blessing. I wanted that for my mother and now that she has passed, I wish that she could have had more time to do so. I wish she had believed in herself. Our path lies ahead of us. It is not yet taken and we have the ability to change its course. Trust that God can get you where you want to go and believe in yourself along the way. You have the power to overcome so long as you live.

The Lotus Pillar

I spent time looking at the women in my family and what they had to go through so that I did not repeat those same experiences and mistakes. Doing so reinforced to me that today is a new day, and I can always do something different. You do not have to stay where you are or focus on the past. As long as you have breath in your body, God is able.

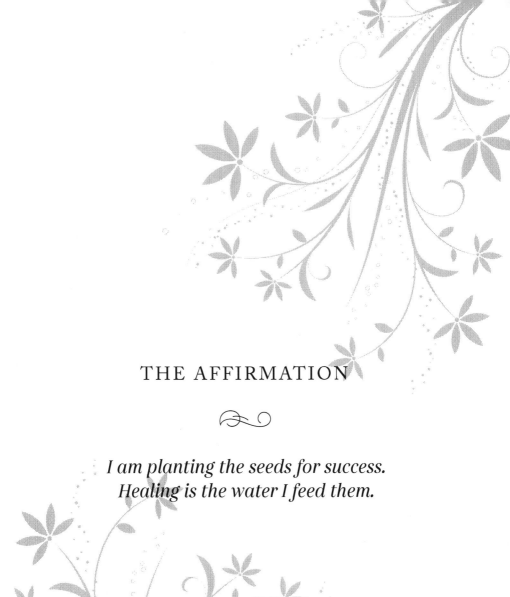

THE AFFIRMATION

I am planting the seeds for success.
Healing is the water I feed them.

NOTES

Pillar 10:

Seeing Life In A New Light

"I like to think of myself as victorious and not a victim. I am a survivor."
∽ Leah Angel Daniel ∽

The Story

Just before middle school, before finally being removed from our mother's custody, we moved into a neighborhood that was beyond questionable. It was a depreciated neighborhood on the east side of Buffalo, New York. It was a drug-infested environment that reminded me of the movie *New Jack City*. The people in the area were so lost to their drug use they looked like zombies. Drug dealers crowded the corner stores and the outside commotion caused me to plug my ears. It was a totally different setting for us from where we used to live on the west side of Buffalo. We saw things that children should not ever see. It was during this time that the little seeds of greatness in me received the nourishment they needed to make me who I am today. In our apartment, this woman who lived upstairs from us, who we called Ms. Geneva. She was a woman of values and morals who had a number of children herself. She knew my mom would leave us by ourselves and must have become tired of always seeing us left home alone. My sister and I were there taking care of ourselves as we lived without guidance. One day she asked my mother if she could take us to Bible school. I was super excited. It was a chance to get out of that house and that neighborhood. Being in a different environment gave me back part of my youth.

At church, I was able to be around kids my age. I did not have to take on the responsibilities of adults. The members of the church were so invested in making sure my sister and I had what we needed. They were the people I wanted to be around. I was able to be a child there and have adults finally provide the safety and security I needed. That is what church became for me. It was a safe and secure escape. The love shown to me through church members affirmed that people did actually care and adults *could* be trusted. Even when we were taken away from our mother, they did not forget about us or throw us away. Designated people in the church were assigned to pick my sister and me up on Sundays. One particular person was Uncle Hank, who took me under his wing and monetarily helped me. He made sure that if there was a trip to be paid for, it was covered. But it was not just about the money. He made sure that I came to church on time and connected with the right people. Others, such as the mother of my twin friends, helped me with fashion. Even the pastor looked out for my sister and me. I remember the day when Pastor DuBois drove in the dead of winter to pick us up. On our way to church, his car broke down, but he did not stress and he did not regret taking that drive. I could not help but think that if I ever got a lot of money, I was going to buy that man a new car because he was just that dedicated and made sacrifices for us to get to church. No matter what foster home we ended up at, he made sure we were at church every Sunday. It was those little things that motivated me to want to be there and be involved. Anything that the church was doing I attended. From singing in a choir to ushering, Leah Angel was there. I enjoyed it and appreciated it as a way for me to stay connected to these amazing people. It was a time for me to get away from my reality and walk in a new vision for my life. I did not know about God or church because that was not how I grew up. But these individuals, who did not know who I was, accepted me and gave me a new chance and an opportunity to learn on my own. The love I was shown and the all-around experience of being involved with the church sparked a desire to engage in activities, which I did throughout my education.

One thing my mother got right was teaching me to be studious. From the time I was a little girl, She instilled in me that education was important. There were many moments in my life when my mother was truly proud of me, but I have one memory of getting good grades in school when I was much younger. My mom bought a cake for me. We were lying on the floor of our apartment eating snacks, and I was playing with a baby doll. My mother told me just how proud she was of me. She was a stickler with education because she was very smart herself. She wanted me to do well, but she didn't take the time to help me get there as I grew older. She pushed me but didn't aid me in my journey. It was on me to figure out how to succeed and then she would take credit for it afterward. It was hurtful, but it did not stop me from enjoying my journey of self-discovery through arts and education.

I was always a very outgoing person, so I wanted to be involved. In middle school, I joined a lot of clubs and played sports. As I became engaged in the different activities, I was able to interact with adults more than my peers. I enjoyed that because I learned a lot from the adults. I was on a drill team, and I loved acting. Speaking in front of people and acting allowed me to be somebody other than who I was. I also enjoyed being around other people who shared similarities with me. When it came to my teachers, they spoke life into me. They saw things in me that I didn't see within myself. They talked to me about the possibilities, the things I could do, and the potential I had to achieve anything I set my mind to. These interactions gave me a glimmer of hope. I realized that I could be more than what other people who spoke negativity into my life believed I could be. I was inspired to interact with people who wanted to do something different in life. I wanted to show my mom that we could steadily do better and that all of us were not products of our environment. I wanted to prevail, which to me was escaping from the drug use and prostitution that was prevalent in my family. I did not want to be a statistic or a Black girl lost stereotype. I was always looking to break free from that generational normality that hindered my family, and those different positive activities that I became involved in gave me that opportunity. I was able to let my guard down and not feel judged. I could spread my wings and see a world outside of what I was born into. I wanted to go to college to get exposed to a different atmosphere where the people were diverse. I loved that and I wanted to be a part of that, yet I never thought I would pursue a doctorate. I never even believed I would pursue and achieve getting a master's degree. I am proud of my accomplishments.

I was excited to transition to college. I was nervous as well, which was why I did not go too far. I still wanted familiarity. Unfortunately, I knew that holding on to anything I did not have to would only stop me from living in God's purpose for my life. I was originally going to attend at the regular start date like everyone else, but life's circumstances changed my decision. The man I was dating at the time, however, was also dating an older woman who began to harass me severely. One day, I could no longer deal with it anymore. On the day before my high school graduation, her harassment was relentless. She continuously called my phone to the point where every ounce of patience in my body dissipated, and I decided to egg her house and throw paint on it. The big bad woman was no longer big and bad as she called the police on me and I was taken to the police station, almost missing my high school graduation. That was the catalyst that made me leave for college early.

I attended college during the year 2000 at a predominantly white institution as an Educational Opportunity Program student. The educational institution I attended was working to diversify its campus, so there were many students from New York City. One young lady would take a special place in my heart and hold it safely, even to this day. Her name is Jennifer Johnson. She was my first friend on campus. Our connection was automatic. While I was from New York, Buffalo proved to be much different from the Big Apple. They teased me about my accent and the way it reminded them of the folks from down South, even though they, too, have their own unique way of speaking. Regardless, I still connected with great people. That was the significance of attending college. It was not so much about the education but the connections and bonds I made as I built a new community.

The Lesson

None of us is exempt from heartache. Though it often doesn't feel like it, we have more control than we think, even in difficult situations. We have power in how we take circumstances and what we shape them into. Do not allow yourself to be restricted by the expectations people place on you or how people treat you. Take your life by the reins and do not give in to the pressures that surround you. Going to college taught me this.

I remember my family members saying, "Oh, you think you're white. You think you are better than everybody because you went to college?"

Those were the words they directed at me. They did not encourage me but rather made sarcastic remarks about what I was doing on campus. I decided that instead of letting their unpleasant words discourage me, I would take my younger family members to campus with me and expose them to what I was experiencing. I wanted to show them what college life was about because we were never exposed to that kind of environment. I knew it was important for me to show my little cousins a different side of life.

The Blessing

The blessing from this story is the village that I made for myself while also recognizing the one I was raised in. I did not need to be ashamed of the fabric that I was cut from. Shame is a heavy burden to carry. Having mentors in the church and at school helped change my perspective on so many things. I learned how to forgive. I learned how to embrace. But I also learned how to fight for what I believed I could have or accomplish.

I was able to understand that my parents could not love me the way I wanted them to because they did not receive that love from their own parents. God loved me so much that He provided people in my life who could show me the love I desperately needed. He allowed me to engage with mentors and colleagues who encouraged me to grow and provided the foundational tools I needed to navigate my life successfully.

The Lotus Pillar

I like to think of myself as a survivor and not a victim. I am victorious. A lot of times, when bad things happened, I would dwell on them. I didn't automatically think of all the good things that have come from them. My upbringing was not what I wanted. My parents did not give me what I needed, but from those experiences, I became a woman who grew stronger than ever. I came out triumphant against all that was set to deter and distract me. I can now use my experiences to guide those around me who are in similar circumstances. I can give hope to someone who desperately needs it, just like I needed it when I was a young girl lost.

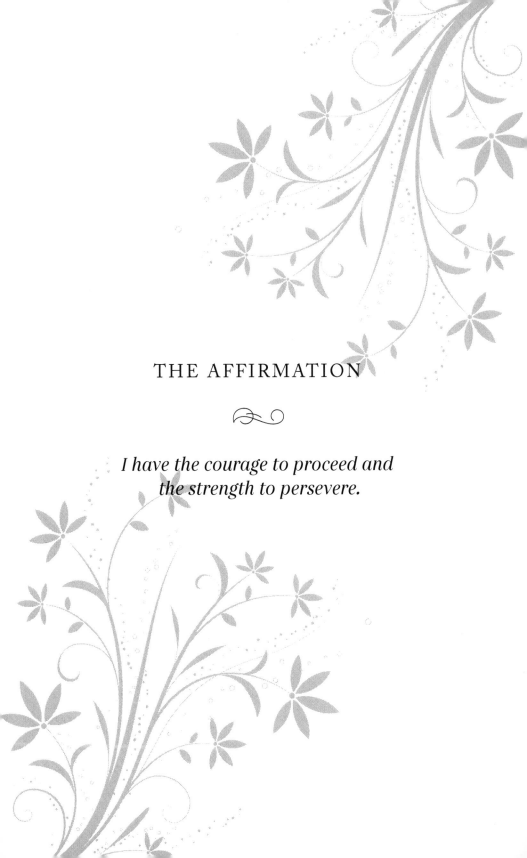

THE AFFIRMATION

*I have the courage to proceed and
the strength to persevere.*

NOTES

NOTES

Pillar 11:

What GOD Has For Me, It Is For Me

"I felt my responsibility was to get him and make the best out of the situation."
~ Leah Angel Daniel ~

The Story

One day I received a concerning call about my brother. I have always been in my siblings' lives. Whatever foster homes or situations they have been in, I have known about it and always assisted in any way possible. This particular brother was adopted and given back twice. He was born with retina deterioration he inherited from his father. It got worse once he started getting into drug use, which accelerated the deterioration. He was burned with hot water by his father's girlfriend when he was one. He was put into group homes and psychiatric institutes where he was violated, so he lived a tumultuous life. When I received that phone call, I began thinking I was in a position where I could take care of him. I had a place to live and a solid job, and I felt I had the love to give him to make him feel better. Looking back, I feel I was naive at that point because I thought if I just gave him love and stability, he would be fine. But he needed so much more. I did not know much about mental health or what he was diagnosed with mentally. I just thought that if he lived with me, a person who truly loved him and could care for him, things would work out because he would be in a better environment. Did I have family members who told me that it wasn't my responsibility and that I should leave him where he was? Absolutely. They did not care despite knowing he had been violated and the trauma he had experienced. They did not care. So I felt it was my responsibility to get him and make the best of the situation.

When I decided to take my brother in, I had to go through a difficult process. I found an apartment in Buffalo, New York, after leaving the foster care system at age 21. I decided to look for a new apartment to allow my brother to be comfortable in his own room. I also had to go through mandatory foster parent and kinship classes. I forged a relationship with his social worker, trying to get as much information as possible about his situation. I soon realized he withheld a lot of information from me, including what happened to my brother while he was in foster care and when he was adopted. My brother's foster care agency was incapable of dealing with the magnitude of his mental health illness. Once he came into my home, I switched him to a different and better-equipped agency. When he finally moved in with me, he came with just the clothes on his back. I had to start anew with my brother and tried to do the best I could. I listened to him. I asked him what had happened, although he wasn't very forthcoming. He had violent outbursts with me, and he performed poorly in school. I would get a call every day from school about him cursing at a teacher or having an outburst, so I would call my mom and tell her that I needed help because I was exhausted. She said she would help me, but that was always on a limited basis. You have to remember I was only 23 years old and had to be a teenager's mother. I did my best to work with him and tried to tell him I understood what he was experiencing. I would tell him that he was a Black man threatening white teachers, and he could not show up like that. I would have him write out the different things he was experiencing or feeling because I wanted him to be able to express his thoughts and have an outlet for his emotions. It was a journey that grew more difficult when I decided to get married, which changed the dynamic again.

The relationship with my first husband was stressful because of my brother living with us. I wanted the best for him, but I was simultaneously trying to leverage a new marriage. In part because of my brother's special needs, he wanted our relationship to continue just being him and me. He had an Oedipus complex, so he would latch on to the dominant female in the home and not want anyone else around.

My brother often would say, "You're just doing that because you got a husband, and you put your husband before me." I felt like he was using that as an excuse for his behavior.

With my first husband, it would be, "You give your brother too many chances. It doesn't matter if he was in foster care. He is taking advantage. Everybody is taking advantage of you."

It was definitely a stressor on the marriage because I was young and had to advocate for my brother. I could not focus on my marriage the way I should have at the beginning, and it took a toll that reached a boiling point when I turned 27. I felt I could no longer care for my brother or get him on the right track. I understood he had every right to be angry, but I didn't want him to get stuck in that mindset for life. I felt like no matter what I did, no matter how many talks I had with him, no matter how many "come-to-Jesus" moments we had, he just didn't get it. I felt like he wanted to stay stuck in his pain.

The end came when he tried to attack me at my home while I was pregnant. I didn't want anyone to harm me, and I didn't want him to get hurt. When I decided to let him go, I was exhausted and didn't have anything more to give. I was disappointed when I decided to give him up, but I wasn't equipped to deal with a legally blind, traumatized young man who would never come to terms with his situation. Toward the end of the road, I found out my brother was using drugs the day I gave him money for a haircut. He came back without a haircut but was high. I was confused about how he gained access to drugs, which I knew were not available in our neighborhood. I realized he was also drinking as I noticed liquor bottles missing from the house. I knew it was time to let him go, so he went back into the foster care system.

I thought that was it. I would see him here and again, but hopefully, he would get the help he needed and a family would be found for him. After he left, accusations arose that he had been physically abused in my house while he was staying with me. I was appalled, especially by the allegations that were insinuated. I couldn't believe that my brother allegedly reported that we had beaten him.

I blatantly told the social worker: "Look at him and me! He is bigger than I am and stronger than I am. There aren't any marks on him. Isn't it apparent that he is lying?"

She told me that she still had to file the report because they didn't want acquisitions of favoritism. After all, it was well-known that I was in the foster care system and personally an advocate.

"We have to treat you the way we treat everyone else," she said.

I was offended that these accusations were being broadcast about me and that anyone would believe I would do such a thing. But I was especially angry at my brother for lying. Given the energy and stock I put into raising my brother and showing him as much love and support as I did, I was pissed to hear that he did this. All of his life, I did nothing but support him and be there for him. I felt that he was very ungrateful and inconsiderate. I was his biggest advocate.

He would later confess his accusations were false, saying, "Oh no, I was lying because I was mad. I felt like she put her baby and husband before me."

I responded, "Do you understand that I could have lost everything I had worked for? You were lying and angry at me because you didn't want to do the right thing."

I didn't feel sorry for him because I had given up so much for my siblings, especially him. Being placed in jeopardy of losing my livelihood and the accomplishments that made me who I am made it impossible for me to feel pity for my brother. From that day, I knew I never wanted to be in that situation again where someone could just disrupt my life, giving no regard to what I had done and sacrificed for them.

If you talked to him today, he would say, "Oh, you know I apologized." I forgave him, but I couldn't come back from that. The damage was done. I can never allow him in my space to jeopardize me in that type of way ever again.

I did not talk to him for many years because I felt offended and hurt. I was an English professor, and I worked with youth. I could have lost my job and would have been unable to provide for myself. Eventually, we began to communicate again, and as a result of my work, I better understood his actions. Ultimately, I realized what I did with him was not wrong or didn't work. I could not succeed because regardless of my efforts and caring, he wanted his parents' love and there was nothing that I could have done to soothe what he felt. Years later, he increased his drug intake and used drugs with our mom. One day I asked him why. Why go down that path after seeing everything that our mom experienced? He admitted that he wanted to know what was so great about the drugs that would make a person give up on their children and their life. That interaction had also given him and our mother an opportunity to bond on a level none of her other kids were willing to experience. My brother was willing to grasp our mother's love and attention by any means necessary.

The Lesson

I learned from my brother's situation that I could not fix everything. At the time I welcomed him into my home, I felt like I could solve any problem thrown my way. I thought my brother was someone who would change his ways and become a model citizen if I gave him my love and attention. He didn't. By the time he moved in with me, he was too far gone for anybody to help him–at least not his sister. He wanted his mom, the woman who had lost custody of him. Every little boy wants his mom, right? For a lot of males, their relationships with their mother teaches them how to treat and love women. He did not have that connection that he desired to have with her. Can you imagine a child constantly fighting for his or her mother's love and attention? Running through life trying to figure out why they love them like other kids are being loved? It's heartbreaking, but the lesson for me is that I have to accept the things that I cannot change despite how distorted they are.

For a long time, I felt I could do no wrong. When I had my brother and saw he was not changing, that affected me because I kept asking myself, "Why?" When he attacked me and lied to me, I was confused. I knew I wasn't perfect, but I thought I could at least fix my brother. I couldn't, and I realized that was okay. I love my brother and my family, but we all have our own demons we are fighting. If we do not wish to defeat those demons on our own, there is little anyone can do to help us. I think that was the best antidote for me to understand. I embraced the truth. I focused on my own life. Change cannot be imposed by the outside world, only by doing the inner work. That lesson bled into my marriage and helped me to feel secure with who I was as an individual, even when failing at something. Just because I didn't get the outcome I wanted didn't mean that something was wrong with me.

The Blessing

The blessing I gained from my experience with my brother is that I learned how to advocate for him and myself. I attempted to do something none of the adults who may have been better equipped attempted to do. I did the best I could with what I had to make my brother's life the best it could be at that moment. My brother had endured so much trauma throughout his life. I often wondered if he would ever recover from some of the things that happened to him.

I no longer feel like it is my responsibility to take on tasks just because no one else steps up to the plate. I assist others because I love empowering them to reach their full potential, but I no longer feel this unbreakable tug to do it and endanger myself or my well-being. When I assist people through my organization or reach out to young people who have transitioned out of the foster care system, I understand that this has become my life's calling but I can only do the best I can and nothing more. If I cannot help someone I am honest, but I also attempt to help them find what they need. I don't think I would have begun to feel this way if I didn't take care of my brother. It may have been a roller coaster that I never wanted to ride again, but it helped show me what I was capable of and what I could not endure. It demonstrated to me that I do not have it all figured out and some things are above me. It also showed me there are times you have to put yourself before others. As I said, no one will look after you more than yourself. I loved my brother, but he was ready to ruin my life with his accusations. His actions showed me that hurt people really do hurt people. From that moment forward, I learned how to be wise, to protect myself, and that some people are beyond my help. This blessing still manifests in my life today.

The Lotus Pillar

When I look back and think about this story with my brother and what I sacrificed, I realize it was a very hard situation. I was resentful and angry at more than just him. I just felt like any time I took my dreams and set them aside, people who I assisted were ungrateful. I felt like I missed out on so much. But believing that what God allows is for me regardless of detours or setbacks means every situation is a set-up for what He has in store for me. The work I do today is a reminder of that. Through every interaction with my brother as I grew up with and raised him, I understood that I needed him in my life so that I could better understand youth and young adults who have mental health diagnoses and how to assist them. I learned so much about the foster care system from his perspective.

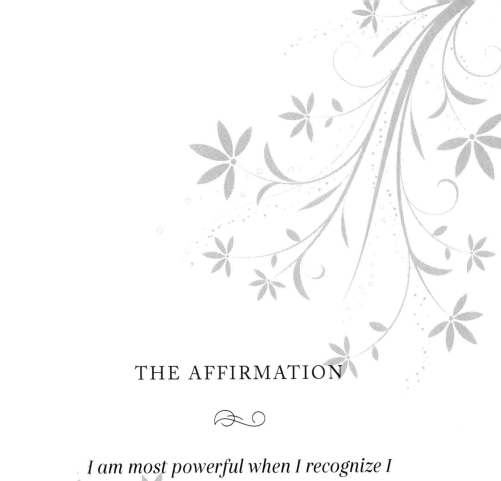

THE AFFIRMATION

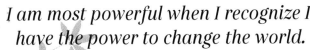

*I am most powerful when I recognize I
have the power to change the world.*

NOTES

NOTES

– 242 –

Pillar 12 :

A Legend Is Born

"My daughter helped me to become more."
Leah Angel Daniel

The Story

Having done so much for others, the last thing I expected was to feel lost and confused in my own life. I knew that others needed help, but I could not assist them when I didn't yet have life figured out for myself. It can be a whirlwind when you realize you are just as human as the next individual and may be more messed up than the person you are working to help. While trying to assist my brother and help him develop into a model citizen, I got married. I thought I could make both relationships work, but it was more difficult than I imagined. I felt pulled in different directions by two people I didn't want to disappoint.

My first husband cheated throughout our entire marriage. I would make excuses for him by saying he was young and would grow out of it. He never did. It reached the point where I was ready to leave him, but that was when I found out I was pregnant. I honestly couldn't believe the timing of it all.

I remember saying, "Oh my God, Lord, you are too funny." It was surreal.

When the initial shock wore off and I thought about what I would do, I contemplated abortion because I didn't want anything to do with my former husband. I was done and didn't want to be a part of the relationship anymore. But I had never been pregnant before, and

I had laid down with this man and the child was my responsibility. I went into deep prayer and knew when I decided to keep the baby that I was choosing to be a single parent because I did not have confidence that my former husband would do the right thing. How do you have faith in someone who has shown you on a repeated basis that he is not committed to you? I tried to do the best I could, but it was reaching the point where it was too mentally exhausting for me to continue in the marriage. I checked out mentally and knew that I would soon leave physically too. Now a baby was being added into the equation. I didn't think that having my child would be the cure for what he and I were going through. I could see he was content with his life despite the pain he delivered to me through his actions and display of blatant disrespect. I didn't want to be with him or have a baby with him, but I was still married to him and pregnant.

When I told him I was pregnant, I accompanied it by saying, "I don't want to do this with you. I don't want to keep the baby." When he heard that, he broke down crying.

He said, "I love you. I will do the right thing. Please keep the baby."

He didn't keep his promise. When I was seven months pregnant, I knew the marriage had completely dissolved. I couldn't even stand to look at him. We weren't intimate, and we no longer pretended even to like one another. I woke up one morning and made up my mind that after I had my baby, she and I would leave. From that point forward, he made my life unbearable. He was always out of town and wasn't paying bills, which stressed me a lot in addition to all that was happening with my brother. My former husband was not supportive of what I was going through, be it the pregnancy or my brother's needs. People may not understand that when you have been the rock for everyone your whole life and things do not work out for you personally, it's traumatic and embarrassing. I was disappointed with myself and the life I chose at that point. Nothing fit with what I thought the outcome would be. My former husband was a first-generation child of an African family. His father was a diplomat who spoke four languages. My former husband saw the world and had done so much, but he still lacked confidence and couldn't seem to find himself.

When it was time for me to have the baby–mind you, this was my first child–my former husband said to me one day, "Well, if the baby does not come this weekend, I am going out of town. I have things to do."

I was like, "Are you kidding me? You have a lot of nerve. I'm not about to do this by myself."

I remember locking myself in the car while we were in the parking lot in front of Sam's Club to get some items we needed before the baby arrived. I cried and was in such disbelief that I was even in such a predicament. I could have married anyone I chose and had a baby, but this is who I picked. I was disgusted. How could I have married this man, let alone laid down with someone who didn't even think enough of me to be there for me and support me? I was disappointed in myself and this major relationship decision in my life, but then I remembered who I was. I said to myself, "Leah get it together. Girl, God's got you and your baby girl." I stopped crying, wiped my face, got out of the car, and purchased what I needed from the store. I needed to let that cry and ugliness out before I bought a new innocent life into this world. I felt a sense of certainty that things would work out for me. When we got home, I sat on the bed, and my water broke. Labor had begun and my reward was on the way. My daughter Legend Sanaa was born a week before Mother's Day. My former husband and I didn't make amends. I went home a few days before Mother's Day, and he went out of town. During my first Mother's Day, I was home taking care of our child while he was out partying with another woman. When I confronted him about it, he had the nerve to tell me he left me a gift, so what was I complaining about?

This was not what I imagined my marriage would be like. I never had a man mistreat me in such a manner, and I was the mother of his child. I was enraged. I couldn't tell anyone how I felt because I would just be ridiculed. At that point, I just knew I didn't have any-body and couldn't depend on anyone else. I realized that just because I was married did not mean I was stable and safe from the harsh realities of life. Having a baby while being married certainly didn't save me from becoming a single parent. It didn't shield me from the different situations single women go through, from having to fight for child support or trying to make a man do right by his child. I was very disappointed because I never thought my life would be like this. I wanted real love, the ride-or-die kind of love where it was my man against the world and me. My life experience quickly changed my perspective about love, marriage, and having children. I was naive enough to believe that I would be different and not be treated like most women. I never thought I would be with someone who was a negligent parent. My ex-husband wanted to hurt me because I left him and he knew that if he didn't take care of our daughter, I would be crushed. That is what I see as a pattern in my life. When I love people, I love profusely. I will do whatever for them. But when they cross me or treat me in a derogatory way, I walk away and treat them as if they don't even exist. How are you upset with me because I will not allow you to use and abuse me? That's crazy. He wanted me to suffer, knowing my heart's desire to have a family of my own. He knew I didn't want to be a single parent but rather to have him in our daughter's life. And yet, here I was, a single, married woman with my five-month old baby, trying to figure out my next steps in life.

I was honestly traumatized by the whole experience. I was grate-ful for my daughter, the most important blessing to come into my life, but I could not believe I had a child with a man who acted the way he did. I decided it was just going to be my baby and me. I clung to Legend, and she clung to me. Even though I was alone, our con-nection was something I had never experienced. I was excited and surprised because of my relationship with my mom, who was not very affectionate. I didn't know what to expect or how I would react to my own child. It was different with my baby and me. I connected with her when she was in utero. When she was born, I loved her. I kissed her, hugged her and held her close to me all the time. Our relationship was something special. I went from being someone unsure if she even wanted to have a child because of my experience with my ex-husband to realizing I could not imagine a world where I did not have her in my life. It helped that I was able to stay home with her for the first two years of her life, as we formed a close relationship that remains today.

The Lesson

The biggest lesson from my daughter's birth and the end of my marriage was the realization that I am not exempt from things happening to me in life. I remember thinking, "Oh, he is not going to cheat on *me* because I am Leah Angel, and I am the bomb," and this and that. I was the woman who thought I would not be a single mom. I did everything right. I had it all figured out. But I realized as a result of the situation with my ex-husband that his actions were all about what he was looking for and where he felt incomplete. His inadequacies led to what he did and didn't have anything to do with me. I realized that it didn't matter how I showed up, how much I loved him, or what I turned a blind eye to. The truth was that I would never be the piece to the puzzle he needed to feel whole.

A burden was lifted from my shoulders when I came to that understanding. I could have spent much more time trying to make my ex-husband who I wanted him to be. He loved his lifestyle and was not trying to settle down with anyone. He had his own problems to deal with, and Legend nor I was going to change him. Of course, I wanted my child to grow up with her father. I always wanted that nuclear family unit. He knew that, but he desired other things. My brother, my ex-husband, and even my mom created moments in my life where I realized that I could not change people and that they had to do the work for themselves. I learned that sometimes it is just best to let them go. I loved them all and wanted the best for them, but if I have to choose between them and me or my child, it will always be Leah and Legend.

The Blessing

My daughter was a blessing in disguise. I didn't don't know much about unconditional love, but I knew that I wanted to give her the world and that I would lay down my life for her. She is my everything. She is the reason I fought so hard when life was unbearable. I wanted to give her the best life, the greatest things that life could offer, and the best opportunities. She gave me a new sense of purpose in life.

When I left my ex-husband, it was just her and me. She was the accelerator in my life. I sometimes wonder what my life would have been like without her. Would I have made different choices? I have no doubt that I would be doing what I am today, but would that same sense of purpose still be there? Would there be that little voice in the back of my mind reminding me that there is a deeper purpose for all of this? I don't know. For her sake, I wish she had been brought into this world under better circumstances. But there is the age-old expression that everything happens for a reason. There was a reason for what I went through and why she came into my life when she did. It was all a part of a bigger purpose, a bigger picture. If I had to thank my ex-husband for anything, it would be for giving me this beautiful little girl because I can no longer imagine my life without her by my side. It brings me to tears just thinking about how much I care about her. I want her life to be filled with her own personal blessings, and I want her to strive to be the best version of herself. This is why I wanted to break the generational curse in my family so that I could provide my own children with a brighter future and guarantee that they would not endure the hardships I went through. Legend is the biggest blessing from my first real relationship heartache.

The Lotus Pillar

When I was pregnant with my first daughter, I watched the movie I Am Legend many times. I could relate to Will Smith's character, who tried to save the world and help everybody by sacrificing himself.

My mother would say, "Leah, you are going to be the one breaking the generational curse in our family."

Guess what? I did and I have! I knew that one day if I birthed a daughter, she would be even greater than I could ever imagine her to be, so when it came to pass that I found out I was pregnant with a girl, I thought it was only appropriate to name her Legend Sanaa. She is someone who is going to do and be extraordinary as a gift to the world and a gift to me. I held on to her to get through that difficult era where I felt disappointed and defeated and wondered how the hell I had gotten myself into this mess, a broken marriage. I hadn't felt such a defeatist status since I was in foster care. I couldn't work or do anything to lift myself out of the situation that I faced at that time. I felt hopeless and not in control. Even though I had those same emotions while in foster care, at least back then, I was a child who had no choice or voice. I didn't have anything or anyone to help me pursue what I wanted to do. As an adult, I had a choice. I didn't have to stay in certain situations. Thank God it only lasted a season and I moved on and designed a life that I could be proud of. Not back into a situation where I wasn't protected and ridiculed. My daughter became my safe space. Her love was all I had to look forward to and empowered me to go forward. I was responsible for someone other than myself, and I would not fail her.

THE AFFIRMATION

*Even through life's struggles, I have the power
to overcome and change my circumstances.*

NOTES

NOTES

NOTES

Pillar 13:

Fostering Greatness

"Turn a negative situation into a positive outcome."
∾ Leah Angel Daniel ∾

The Story

I started my doctoral journey in the fall of 2008. I was an English professor and decided to take the next step in my educational career by pursuing my doctorate in English education. This was the same time that I discovered I was pregnant with my first daughter. Never had I gone to school while having a child, so this was a different experience. I thrived in my doctoral program but continued to be crushed by life. I was nine months pregnant when I broke my wrist in three places at work. The walls around me came crashing down as I thought to myself, "How am I going to complete this program?" I couldn't even write. I decided to take a leave after I had my daughter. This was around the same time I was living with my father and his wife, as well as going through my divorce.

One day a friend of mine said, "I heard about this other doctoral program and it is supposed to be for working professionals."

The program was in executive leadership and classes were held on the weekends about an hour from Buffalo in Rochester, New York. Was this the program God wanted me to pursue? I guess you never know until you take that leap of faith, which is what I did. I enrolled and it was one of the best decisions I ever made. Going through that program, life did not let up. Many trials and tribulations still attempted to overpower me. I remarried and still dealt with the realities of marriage. I thought I knew how to navigate romantic relationships, but the marriage was another mountain to climb. I learned that I connected to men through trauma bonds but thought they would never treat me wrong because I valued myself. Working through problems and life situations with another human being who had different life circumstances than myself was a major challenge. I felt like I was working on myself and I could not take on the burden of other people's lives, but this is what marriage is about. My health was also challenged when I had a breast cancer scare and I was shaken when told I needed cysts removed from my breast. I was scared, nervous, and anxious. I was under the age of 40 so I had to advocate for myself to receive a mammogram. I knew something wasn't normal when I felt a lump that just kept growing, yet I had to convince my doctor to write a script for me to be seen. The lump grew at a concerning rate, and I had a biopsy done. The biopsy was painful and an experience that I will never forget. Finally, the doctor agreed to remove the lump. I am thankful it was noncancerous, but my health challenges continued as I had to have rotator cuff surgery on my right shoulder. All of this occurred while I was a mother struggling to find childcare assistance so that I could pursue my graduate degree on the weekends. I could not believe I was in this situation. I did everything right and life still had a way of showing me that even when we plan, things can still go their own way. When I completed my first two degrees, all I had to worry about was Leah, but now I was Leah, the mommy. I had to make sure this little child had what she needed before I could pursue my educational dream. Mentally, I was not ready. Going through the doctoral program was hard, stressful, and strenuous on my mind, body, and spirit. It was a journey of explaining my path, knowing that each conversation would come with a rebuttal. At times it became discouraging, but an unexpected person provided support, staying close to my ear and offering encouragement. It was my mother. One thing that was consistent in my life was education and how it always helped me to level up. My mother instilled educational values in me from the time I was a young child. I truly appreciated that about her.

She always called me Dr. Leah, which was the motivation I needed. She knew I had the power within me to pursue and finish my doctorate degree. She believed in me. I know that in my heart. Did she have her own way of showing it? Yes, she did. She always put her two cents in on what she believed she contributed, but that was simply her own reminder that she did something good as well. She needed that for herself. When I finally understood the reasons for her actions, I stopped taking the statements personally. I knew that she was not attacking me but rather was patting herself on the back about how out of all the things she did in this world, I was the one *good* outcome. It was painful that she could not see it all come to fruition.

My mother passed on June 14, 2021, as I was preparing for my dissertation proposal defense. Again I had no choice but to step away. I could not push through mentally. Around the time of my mother's death, the COVID-19 pandemic was a growing crisis and I had just delivered another baby girl. My mother was only able to see her a handful of times. This pregnancy came with severe health concerns because I was 38 years old. My pregnancy was considered a geriatric pregnancy and my baby was breech. I was working full-time, suffering from postpartum depression, had two children to care for, and my mother's health was deteriorating. Adding to the pressure was the fact my mother died far away from me in North Carolina. I remember when she shared her plan to move. I was not happy about that because I knew her health was not the best.

"What if something happens to you? How am I going to get to you if you're all the way down there?" That is what I told her, but as usual, she didn't listen to me.

Once again, everything fell on me as I had to take responsibility for my mother's funeral arrangements. I needed to get her body from North Carolina to Buffalo. Only a couple of family members were willing to assist me with the cost. My mother did not have life insurance and the expectation was that I would take care of everything. The family showed out so badly during my mother's funeral. People were lying and reminiscing about what they had done for her when most of them contributed to her drug issue. On top of that, my brother was imprisoned just days before my mother passed away and threatened to harm himself while incarcerated if he was not able to attend the funeral service. All of this stress was a mental trigger I did not need. Getting the documentation to have him attend was another task placed on me. All of my younger siblings were going through their own ordeals and they were unable to support me in any way. The entire process drained me to the point where I was completely tapped out from being overstimulated and utilized. Having to carry this load on my shoulders without a support system resulted in me becoming physically ill. I was on my menstrual cycle for three months straight, which started on the day of my mother's funeral. I was unable to do any of the things I needed to do to take care of myself and my own children. I could not get off the couch because I had no physical energy, but I knew I could not stay in that space. I knew I needed to take steps to heal and be better, which is what I did. I began seeing a therapist and visiting my primary care physician. To my surprise, I discovered I had stress-induced diabetes, high blood pressure after the birth of my youngest daughter, and severe anxiety to the point where I woke in the middle of the night and felt as if someone was sitting on my chest. The weight of the world was crushing me. I needed support, especially with the passing of my mother, and I did not have that.

All I had were the eyes looking in and people saying, "You're the good doctor. You got it. You always take care of everything."

That was the overall sentiment. "*Leah got it!*" I remember when my mother was alive, she too believed that I would make everything alright. There was a time before her passing when she received a settlement of about $12,000.

"Mom, give me some of that money," is what I told her.

"Oh, you got it. I know you have something stashed away."

Just like the rest, she believed I was financially successful and did not need any assistance, but I did! The reality of funeral costs hit me hard, and my mom left it all to be placed on me. It was a lot and I was angry with her. I had told her not to move out of town because she was sick, but she did not listen to me. I knew I could not get to her if something happened, but she did not see it how I saw it and, unfortunately, how I knew it would be what came to pass. I was agitated and upset that I was not with her when she passed. She died around people who did not love her or even know her last name. I was cheated of having closure because I could not be with her during her last moments. I was upset with my family because, even with death, they showed zero concern for me and my well-being. They were selfish and focused on themselves, making the funeral about the issues they had with her before she passed away. They lied and claimed to help her when they did not. Even my friends, who I thought I could count on, who I shared my struggles about my mother with and set high expectations, were nowhere to be found when I needed them. I felt as though I had prepared them before the storm came so they could be by my side and contribute in whatever way they could, but they did not show up. It was once again a harsh reality. My mother died, but no one cared. Nonetheless, I was grateful she did not suffer and that I did have the financial means to travel to North Carolina and see her body and bring her back to Buffalo despite it putting me in a very compromising situation with my own monetary responsibilities.

The Lesson

Losing a parent is more difficult than anyone could ever imagine, especially when you hold on to the hope that they will one day be everything you desire them to be. It was hurtful to know my mother's journey was over. She would never get the opportunity to live the fulfilled life that I thought she should experience before she left this earth. That was hurtful because I did not want that life just for my mother but for us, her children. I wanted her to have the chance to mend the relationships with her younger children and grow with her grandchildren. It was not just about me. It was about the healing that could have occurred if she had been in a different state of mind and lived a different way. My siblings yearned for that. They often talked about the conversations they could have had with her. They did not get that opportunity the way I did. They never truly got to know her. They were all hurt in their own way and even took that hurt out on me.

At the funeral, my sister stood up in front of the family and said, "We all know Leah was mommy's favorite."

It frustrates me to know they feel that way. My relationship with my mom was different than my siblings. Out of all of us, I was the one who was not a drug-addicted baby. I was born into wedlock and I was planned. I know that reality was hurtful for them. I was the reminder of what she wanted to be and what she was able to get right. They did not see that because they were hurting, and rightfully so. They could only see how she rejected them. They remembered the things she did with them and to them that a mother should not have done. That was all they could see, and they wanted to be able to have something more meaningful.

The Blessings

I am my mother's legacy. She let me know she was proud of me. She let me know I am the prize. When it comes to my siblings, there are still holes I know they wish were filled and loose ends that weren't tied the way they needed to be to provide closure for them. While I wanted the outcome of my relationship with my mother to be different, I do not have any regrets about the relationship as a whole or who I was to her and who I showed up to be in her life. I was proud of my mother because she was clean when she died as a result of her liver and other organs shutting down. The toxicology report showed she had no drugs in her system. That was a blessing I needed to hear.

The Lotus Pillar

When you take the good, bad, ugly, shame, hurt, joy, pride, and love and shape it into what you as an individual want it to be–knowing that at the end of the day, it makes up who you are–that creates greatness in you. Fostering is putting it all together. Greatness is you and me. It is us, with everything that we come with. It all makes us who we are. All that I have been through has made me into who I am. I embrace my greatness.

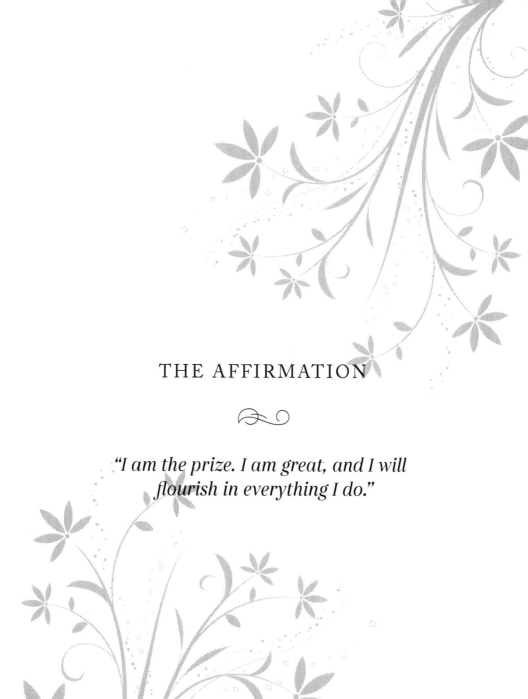

THE AFFIRMATION

*"I am the prize. I am great, and I will
flourish in everything I do."*

NOTES

NOTES

Pillar 14:

Dear Little Leah Angel

"You are her legacy. Never forget that."
～ Leah Angel Daniel ～

Dear Little Leah Angel,

I just want to let you know that it is okay to be who you are. You go girl. Love yourself. Your mom truly loves you. She did the best she could with what she had. You are her legacy, never forget that. Leah Angel, God has truly blessed you abundantly and exceedingly. Never forget that you are special. Never forget that you are the one who has made a way for others. You are the example and that isn't anything negative. It is something that you should always be proud of. You do not have to be ashamed about making decisions and things not working out the way you planned. Baby girl, that's life. Unpredictable, but still worth living. Just flourish and shine and be who you are. Listen, you know that when you finish doing the work and leave this earth, all that you have done will be appreciated and it will live on through your two daughters, Legend Sanaa, Jewel Penelope ,and every individual you have touched. You are amazing in every way, baby girl. Remember that and walk in that with confidence. You are who you were meant to be. The truth needs no defending.

With Love,
Leah Angel Daniel

The Lesson

Some of us just make the best of what we have and never complain, but some of us just want more than what we were given. Often we are on the outside looking in at others, labeling them as being dysfunctional. What we see as dysfunction, however, is often normalized behavior based on our generational makeup. We frequently judge what we do not understand. This is typical human behavior, but now it's time for each of us to be part of the solution and not part of the problem. It is time to heal, grow and thrive. This book has allowed me to create a space where I can share part of my story and for you to walk this path with me. Sharing our stories reinforces how we can forgive and give grace even when we are leaving one season of life and transferring to another.

The Blessings

Knowing that my mother believed I was her rock and the one she could always trust to be there for her meant the world to me. It was a blessing and a burden. Knowing how she felt about me filled a hole in my heart that Little Leah needed to have closed. My mother knew I would take care of things, and I believe it brought her peace. She knew she was safe and secure with me. Ironically, I was able to give both to her despite still searching for safety and security for myself after not having either in my life. I was able to give my mother love, grace, understanding, and forgiveness. All that she needed to feel whole.

The Lotus Pillar

My mother called me two days before she passed away, and we had the best conversation. We were laughing and talking about anything and everything. Before we hung up, she spoke words that I had longed to hear my entire life.

She said, "I love you, Leah, and I just want you to know that I appreciate everything you have done for your siblings and me. You are doing everything that I was supposed to do, and I am so proud of you. Take care of my kids. They need you. You know you are the only one with good sense, lol."

Her words were like a soft symphony to my ears. My mother never fully apologized for losing my siblings and me to foster care or for me sacrificing my youth to care for them. And yet reflecting on the journey I experienced with my mom, I felt complete satisfaction. I felt a sense of respect for her that I had never experienced before. It reignited the hope that was lost on the day she missed my baby shower for Jewel. I found myself setting new and greater expectations for her. I wanted her to be able to live the type of life she desired to live. I realized that my mother always did things on her own terms, but she also instilled something great in me. She taught me that being who she was–her addiction and battling schizophrenia–did not fully define her. Her life meant so much more. Realizing that made me want to show her some kind of appreciation that I could not express when she was living. I know that my mother knew I loved her. She knew I made many sacrifices, and it meant so much to me that she did indeed appreciate every one of them.

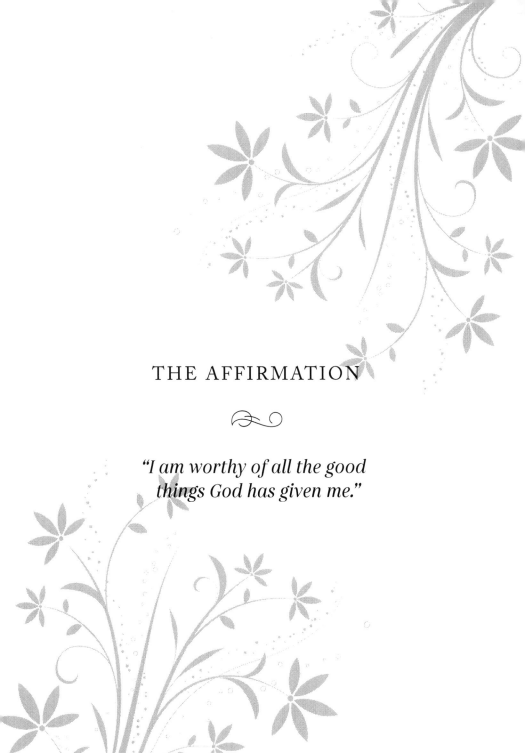

THE AFFIRMATION

*"I am worthy of all the good
things God has given me."*

NOTES

NOTES

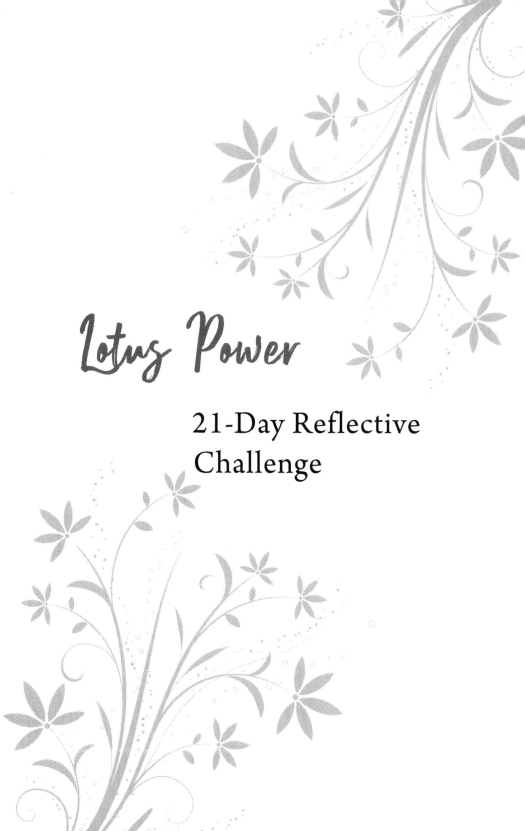

Lotus Power

21-Day Reflective Challenge

W elcome to the Lotus Power Challenge! Below you will find a list of 21 journal prompts that will help you in your healing and self-discovery journey. Challenge yourself to complete one prompt a day until you've completed the list. Take time to reflect on each prompt and consider how you can incorporate healing into your daily life.

1. Make a list of 10 affirmations for yourself. They can be professional or personal. Keep that list where you can see it each day.

2. List your greatest strengths and weaknesses. Reflect on them. How do you utilize your strengths in your career and day-to-day life? How can you turn your weaknesses into strengths?

3. What are your immediate and long-term goals? What steps do you need to take to achieve them? Are the people around you supportive of these goals and the process to obtain them? If not, how can they become a better advocate for you?

4. Make a list of the things you value most in life in order of importance. Then make a second list ranking how you currently value them. Are the two lists similar or different? If they are different, why do you think that is? How can you prioritize the values you view as more important?

5. What events in your life impact you to this day? If they are traumatic events, how have you worked to overcome the

existing trauma? If you are still on your healing journey, how can you work toward loosening trauma's grip?

6. How do you feel about setting boundaries? Are there boundaries you've had to set in your life? Are there boundaries you feel you still need to set? What steps can you take to do so?

7. What is your current greatest challenge? What are the steps you have taken or need to take to overcome it?

8. Do you feel fulfilled in your professional life? How about your personal life? Reflect on why you feel that way.

9. What are your favorite self-care activities? How can you incorporate these into your daily routine?

10. What is your favorite childhood memory? How do you carry that childlike joy with you into adulthood?

11. Make a list of your greatest fears. Reflect on how they hold you back, as well as make you stronger.

12. Write down your top five favorite qualities about yourself. Now ask someone you care about what their favorite qualities about you are. How do they compare? How do the similarities and differences make you feel? Reflect on this.

13. Do you hold grudges? What are they, and why do you think you're still holding on? Are there any steps you can take to begin to let go?

14. Do you ever feel like others have expectations of you that are unfair, unrealistic, or unjust? Write about how these expectations make you feel. How do these expectations impact the choices you make?

15. What is the strongest emotion in your life right now? Write about why you've been feeling this way.

16. Write a letter to your child self. What would you like them to know?

17. Write a letter to your future self. Write about your aspirations and some advice you think you'll need.

18. What is a habit you'd like to have? Building a habit requires time and practice. How can you incorporate this habit into your daily routine?
19. Who are the people closest to you? What qualities do they have that make them invaluable?
20. Describe your happy place. What does it look like? How does it make you feel? Is it a real space from your past or present, or a place you like to imagine yourself in? Who is allowed in that space?
21. Describe what your life would look like if you were at perfect peace. What do you need to accomplish that? Begin a new journey, one that is driven toward that goal.

Congratulations on completing the Lotus Power Challenge! Be proud of how far you have come in just 21 days. Continue to practice mindfulness and journaling into the future so that you may present every day as your best self.

Lotus Power Playlist

The Only Approval I Need Is My Own.
〜 Leah Angel Daniel 〜

1. *Grwn Woman* — A.I. the Anomaly (feat. B. Angelique)
2. *Another Statistic* — Ace Hood
3. *Devil Get Off Me* — Ace Hood
4. *Can't Give Up Now* — ChoSon (feat. Darcel Blue)
5. *I Love My Life* — Demarco
6. *Nobody But God* — Dorinda Clark-Cole
7. *Take It Back* — Dorinda Clark-Cole
8. *Again* — Faith Evans
9. *Closer* — Goapele
10. *This Is Me* — Kierra Sheard
11. *Toast* — Koffee
12. *Unstoppable* — Koryn Hawthorne
13. *Here I Am* — Marvin Sapp
14. *Amazing* — Mary J. Blige

JOIN US AS WE CHANGE THE NARRATIVE FOR FOSTER YOUTH, YOUNG ADULTS, AND ALUMNI.

To learn more about Fostering Greatness and how you can save our youth from being homeless, visit www.fosteringgreatnessinc.org.

Fostering Greatness needs you! Help support foster care youth, young adults, and alumni by donating at https://givebox.com/fosteringgreatnessinc.

Your contribution will assist foster youth with access to community support and opportunities such as skills training, mentoring, and other resources to help empower alumni to live full, sustainable, and successful lives.

About the Author

I shouldn't be here. I shouldn't be successful. An alumni of the foster care system, a mother often in prison and on drugs, and an absentee father, the statistics would suggest my success was unlikely – an aberration even. Let me share with you how I fostered my greatness!

Storytelling and sharing have inspired me to find my own way. With resilience, faith, and incredible mentors along the way, I first obtained my Bachelor's Degree in Communications, Broadcasting & Mass Media, then a Master's in English while working as an English Professor. In addition to penning this book, I am currently

completing my Doctoral Degree in Executive Leadership. My dissertation focuses on African American women who experienced foster
care and identify as transformational leaders. My focal point, like
the one you'll find in the pages of this book, is post-traumatic healing and growth. Additionally, as the Founder of Fostering Greatness
Inc. (2019), I have assisted hundreds of young adults and foster care
alumni of color to succeed despite the many challenges that they
have faced along the way. As an "Alumna of the foster care system,"
I work toward ensuring young adults leaving the foster care system
see a clear path ahead for themselves, a path that leads to success.

I am a wife, mother, educator, advocate, and believer. My life
experiences have given me an innate desire to give back to the community that raised me; this is what fuels me.

CONNECT WITH LEAH ANGEL DANIEL ON SOCIAL MEDIA

@leahangeldaniel